The Cyclist's Bible

The Cyclist's Bible

Al Sagazio with Robert Elman

DOUBLEDAY
NEW YORK LONDON TORONTO SYDNEY AUCKLAND

PUBLISHED BY DOUBLEDAY
a division of Bantam Doubleday Dell Publishing Group, Inc.
1540 Broadway, New York, New York 10036

Doubleday and the portrayal of an anchor with a dolphin
are trademarks of Doubleday, a division of Bantam
Doubleday Dell Publishing Group, Inc.

Library of Congress Cataloging-in-Publication Data

Sagazio, Al, 1963
    The cyclist's bible/Al Sagazio with Robert Elman.—1st ed.
        p.   cm.
    ISBN 0-385-47304-4
    1. Cycling.   2. Bicycles.   I. Elman, Robert.   II. Title.
GV1041.S16   1995
796.6   dc20   94-49550
                                            CIP

May 1995

10   9   8   7   6   5   4   3   2   1

First Edition

Contents

Acknowledgments

The authors would like to thank the following people and organizations:
>   Bethlehem Photo Graphics in Bethlehem, Pennsylvania
>   Genesis Bicycles in Easton, Pennsylvania
>   Lou's Bicycle Center in Seminole, Florida
>   Suncoast Cycle Center in Pinellas Park, Florida
>   Bill Daley
>   Catie, Dan, and Tom Elman
>   Nancy Hofmann
>   Jennifer and Dean Jones
>   Alfred Sagazio, Sr.
>   Lisa Schmiege
>   Nancy Neely, Lois Brown, and the Lehigh County
>   (Pennsylvania) Velodrome
>   Kathy Koberlein, for helping to start the project.

Photo Credits

Jody Brunner, page 144
Burley Design Cooperative, page 13, 146 (top)
Cannondale Corporation, page 131 (bottom)
Donna Chiarelli, page 15
Bill Daley, pages 36, 37, 41, 43, 60, 69, 70, 76, 81, 91,
        93, 97, 98, 137
Tom Elman, pages 48, 54, 56, 84, 117, 158
Janice Hoffman, page 62
Edwin Landrock, page 149
Lehigh County Velodrome, page 152
Joe Marcus, page 148
Mike Randolph, pages 146 (bottom), 147, 155
Al Sagazio, Sr., pages 57, 127, 159 (top)

All other photos by the authors.

Introduction

It's any bright June Sunday. A father, mother, and son, wearing colorful spring attire and bright helmets, coast to a picnic bench overlooking a valley. I'm seated on the next bench, watching, sweat dripping from my nose in beads because I've just set a new personal best time for racing up this mountain. I wave to the family and they return the greeting with friendly smiles. Bicycles are just machines, yet they link people in the same way that sports cars link strangers on the road. When I see other cyclists, I see comrades. I watch, remembering when I began cycling, and think that's how my father and brother and I look even now when we ride together. It may be the only time we don't argue, or if we do it's playful. The people at the neighboring picnic bench pull out lunch, and so do I.

Bike. The word elicits an image of a kid's plaything. If you think about it, you may picture a marvelously simple machine so efficient it's perfect for kids. But its simplicity and economy make it an ideal multipurpose conveyance for adults, as well—and you might say this simplicity has been somewhat "adulterated" only by the demand for versatility.

Modern bikes are indeed versatile. Today a bicycle can play a major part in any reasonable fitness program. A kid can get together with his best friend to ride bikes for recreation or transportation. Much money has been earned by racing a bicycle faster and farther than the next man or woman. You can cycle through mud, if you're so inclined, on a machine beautifully designed for cycling through mud. The Chinese are famous for the countless bicycles they use to conduct their daily business; even Americans, with their penchant for cars, are commuting more and more by bicycle. Merchants once pulled their carts with bicycles, and a few still do. The police have enforced the law with bicycles, and it was a bicycle organization that pressed for better roads in this country.

Bicycles have often been used by military couriers. There is no evidence that they were ever ridden in battle, but they came very close during World War II. On June 6, 1944—D-Day—some Canadian troops carried bicycles as they waded ashore on the Juno Sector of the Normandy beaches. Assigned the role of a sort of modern light cavalry detachment, they had a special mission: to speed along the road to a German strong point, at Caen, that had to be taken. Unfortunately, the beachhead fighting was so fierce that the bicycles immediately became an encumbrance. Every man had to proceed on foot while using both hands to carry and fire a weapon. "We dumped our bicycles and marched south," one of them recalled. Bicycles are far better suited to the joys of peace than the horrors of war.

Bicycles have evolved into specialized vehicles to accommodate today's specialized world. Twenty years ago, the untrained eye was forced to look for racks and sturdy tires in order to tell a touring bike from a racing bike. Today we have three readily distinguishable, basic types of bikes.

During the early 1980s, the whole country seemed to plunge into a health and fitness craze. Many people bought bicycles with the idea of getting into shape by tooling around their neighborhoods. That was how the mountain bike gained such popularity; novice riders saw the upright handlebars and thick tires and thought: "Now there's a comfortable bike. No more straining my back in contorted positions just so I can go faster." This logic prevails today among many riders and is acceptable (not really right, but acceptable) provided the rider will remain a casual cyclist, with no interest in further bicycle activities. I don't mean to sound snobbish about casual riding. It's a boon to all cycling, and the more specialized activities would be far less advanced if casual cycling weren't so popular.

This book begins with casual riding and the bicycles suited to that use—and even if you've been riding a bike since early childhood you're likely to find some very helpful information.

Thorough coverage will also be devoted to specialized bicycles and riding activities—road touring, all-terrain cycling, and the various forms of racing. There's real adventure in all of these activities; except for advanced racing, any healthy, physically fit person can participate.

And now, come on along. After riding with us through these pages, you'll be a better cyclist whether you choose to cycle casually around town or seek more distant adventures.

1

The Bikes

The quality of bicycle you'll ultimately need depends on how seriously you intend to cycle. The distance you want to ride has little to do with it, but you can't truly increase your speed without being somewhat dedicated. Any safe department-store bicycle is more than acceptable for tooling around the neighborhood. Enter a race with that same bicycle and you'll finish the race (assuming you can ride the distance), but you may not fare well in the standings.

There are three basic types of bikes: touring bikes, racing bikes, and the newcomers, all-terrain bikes (ATBs), also called mountain bikes. If we compare cars and bikes, the touring bike is the Cadillac, the racing bike is the Ferrari, and the ATB, the Jeep. These are the dedicated bikes, and you can't often buy one for less than $600—purists will say the figure is much higher. But don't be alarmed. Most bikes are compromises, just as are most cars. Understanding the extremes will help you understand the compromises. After all, it's the extremes that are compromised.

TOURING BIKES

What often is called a "touring bike" is a bike whose dimensions and habits fall somewhere in between a racer and a true touring bike, similar

1

to a mid-sized car passing for a luxury car. We're going to discuss "real" touring bikes in this section.

A road-touring bike is a big-looking thing. It doesn't have the sleek, bare, sterile look of a racing bike, nor quite the rugged, confrontational face of an ATB. It does have a fairly rugged appearance, though, and is more ready than gangly. Ready—like it's waiting for something; ready to carry things; ready for long, steady riding; ready to gently mingle with pacific country roads and endure punishment from angry streets.

The differences aren't just a matter of appearance. The chainstays are at least 17 inches long on a real touring bike, and the wheelbase can exceed 42 inches. The head- and seat-tube angles are shallower than on a racing bike. Trail and rake are increased. Rims are beefy and tires wide, when compared to a mere road bike that isn't a touring model. All this technical jargon (which we'll discuss later in the chapter) says the bike will have a softer, more relaxed ride. Admittedly, the bike is more hesitant to make changes—it won't fight you, but you mosey rather than swerve around potholes.

Tooling around at the seashore doesn't require an expensive or elaborate bike. This single-speed, coaster-brake relic, complete with basket and rack, easily transports its owner to an afternoon swim. And it's less likely to be stolen.

Add camping gear to a touring bike like this Cannondale model and it's ready for any trip. The front and rear racks, long chainstays, and fenders enhance comfort and versatility. The cantilever brakes can easily and efficiently stop a fully loaded touring bike, and the triple chainring helps tame long, steep hills. A touring model of this general type costs $750 to $1,500, depending on components and accessories.

Touring is a direct extension of casual riding. Appropriately, the touring bike is an extended casual bike. It's a little longer, a little wider, a little smoother—a little more of everything—like a Cadillac is a little more car than an ordinary passenger car.

A touring bike has a wide gear range. Its triple chainring provides very low gears so you can easily climb steep grades while loaded down with survival necessities. Muscling up hills without help from a low gear is needlessly laborious, and no one is as strong as he thinks he is on the fourth day of a hilly tour, especially when lugging an extra 15 to 25 pounds up hill after hill.

A touring bike is equipped with drop-style "racing" handlebars. Although you can cheat the wind with these bars, the real advantage is that they offer five hand positions. (Try driving your car for two hours

Drop-style handlebars are good for more than cheating the wind and going fast—they offer these five different hand positions, which are necessary for comfort and efficiency, especially on long rides. The cycling computer near the center of the handlebar is handy for measuring speed, distance, and elapsed time.

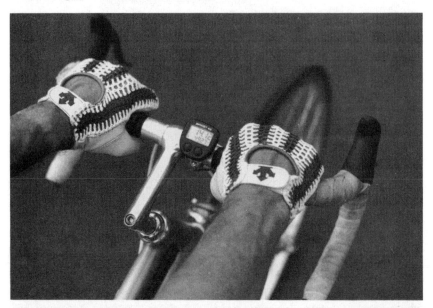

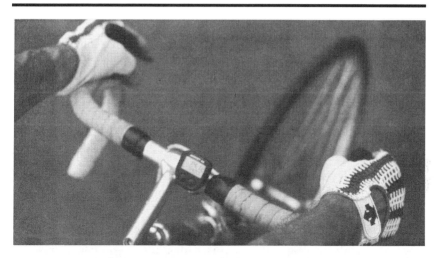

without changing your hand position on the steering wheel.) When they're properly adjusted, these bars *improve* your comfort level.

RACING BIKES

Racing bikes are the antithesis of touring bikes. They're short and compact with steep angles that make them quick and exciting, creating a busy ride sometimes bordering on nervous. A racing model's stiffness allows every ounce of energy you apply to the pedals to get to the road. The wheels sport narrow tires, often less than an inch wide, and fewer spokes reduce weight and wind resistance.

The gearing is completely different, too. The total range is much narrower, with the gears spaced closer together so you can choose the exact gear to match your strength and cadence for the given terrain. You sacrifice the super-low gears for climbing monster hills, but you're climbing on the road and without a load, and the wheels and bike are feather-light, the tires narrow and filled with high air pressure, so friction and momentum loss are lower than with the ATB or the tourer. Besides, a racer wants as little weight as possible— super-low "granny" gears add weight with the extra chainring, larger rear cogs, larger derailleurs, and a longer chain. Mechanical complexity can be the greatest weight of all, and can speel the loss of a race if a crucial shift fails.

The racing bike's sleeker riding position makes you more aerodynamic, distributes your weight more evenly between your hands and seat, and allows for a more efficient use of your glute (buttock) muscles. Those drop-style handlebars aren't designed to give you a sore back, and, when properly adjusted, they won't. They do offer those wonderful five hand positions, a real boon on longer rides.

Riding a racing bike is fun, but don't equate this kind of fun with comfort. A Ferrari can be great fun to drive, but nobody drives a Ferrari across the country because it's comfortable.

A racing bike positions your body to be very aerodynamic by keeping you low and flat. My back can be relatively flat even when my hands are on top of my drop handlebars. The new "aero" handlebars position your arms in front of your body so you don't act like a sail. Your forearms rest on pads while your hands grasp the front part of the bars. They take some getting used to because you're "steering" from the center of your

Here are two solid road-racing bikes that are suitable for other kinds of fun besides racing. Author Al Sagazio uses a bike comparable to either of these as his road bike. Compare them to the touring model (shown in another photo) and you'll notice that racing bikes have a shorter chainstay and derailleur cage, narrower gear range, and "sleeker" appearance. The Cannondale road-racing model (top) has a 45cm frame, designed for small riders; the other model, by Trek, has a 56cm frame, which is about average. Bikes of this type may cost anywhere from $600 to $3,000.

These cyclists are demonstrating good, relaxed form, with no strain on arms, legs, or back. This is made possible because they are riding bikes that fit them properly. They are neither too cramped nor too extended, so they can maintain a natural riding position.

handlebars, so you have less control. But these bars are fast, and with some practice you can soon get used to them.

MOUNTAIN BIKES

When a confident person gets an idea, he listens politely to the dissenters, but continues about his business, and lets the result speak for itself. Remember what "made in Japan" used to mean? The Japanese never said a word, but quietly inched closer and closer to American standards, and then suddenly, one day, the "standards" were no longer good enough. The mountain bike took over in this manner.

We were skeptical at first, maybe even afraid. And then, very quietly, the tidal wave came. Mountain bikes grabbed the bike world and snapped it, as you'd snap a towel when you take it off the clothes line. Their designers rearranged, discarded, added, and invented something that was everything a modern bike wasn't supposed to be.

The result sits upright, has wide, soft tires, and isn't the least bit daunted by potholes, curbs, rocks, or even the unexplored backwoods. Today's ATBs have gears ranging from near the highest high to lows lower than those normally reserved for three-year tours through the Alps via the Himalayas. Some even have shock absorbers. They don't try to cheat the wind, and aren't even made for riding fast. Or are they? They can be, but for riding fast "somewhere else," somewhere taboo for road bikers.

A classic mountain bike. A wide gear range includes super-low gears for climbing soft, steep hills that may present the added challenge of rocks and logs. The wide, low-pressure tires provide traction and cushion the rider from jolts. The stretched-out frame makes the bike very stable. Bicycles like this Trek model are priced between about $300 and $600, though some sophisticated ATBs (all-terrain bicycles) with costly components and accessories cost as much as $3,000.

A fully suspended mountain bike (featuring front and rear shock absorbers) provides extra control and comfort when the trail gets rough. Normally, the fork's bend absorbs shock; on this Cannondale bike, with a straight fork, that's the front shock's job. The rear shock contributes to this and also helps to keep the rear wheel in contact with the ground. Fully suspended mountain bikes cost between $900 and $3,000.

Mountain bikes are everything a modern bike isn't supposed to be because they're meant for different kinds of riding. They can take you to a secret place, like the one you had as a kid, the one only you and your best friend knew about. If you don't have a secret place, a mountain bike can help you find one. Riding a mountain bike can be therapeutic because you needn't worry about where you're headed. Where you're going is where you wind up. And when you're ready to go back to the real world, the mountain bike is ready to take everything the real, harsh world can give.

These bikes really are rugged. They quietly cope with smooth towpaths and noisy city streets, but you can't fully appreciate them until you tackle rocky trails with one. Of course, you must increase your skills to find the limits of the bike—I know I have a long way to go before I reach the limits of the ATB I've been riding for the last year or so.

A mountain bike has a stretched-out frame for stability. Its higher clearance (bottom-bracket height) helps keep the bike off rocks and fallen tree trunks that lie across your trail. The step-over height, though, is lower, because sometimes you have no choice but to get off the bike in a hurry, and the last thing you want then is the top tube coming fast at your crotch. The wide, knobby tires work on uneven terrain the way a snowshoe works on snow, or a mud tire works in mud. The lower air pressure in these tires helps soak up bumps. The bike has the low gears for climbing steep, rocky trails. The upright handlebars put you in an upright position for more efficient climbing and absorbing impact with your arms. Cantilever brakes stop the bike authoritatively. It truly deserves the moniker "all-terrain bicycle."

Another virtue of the mountain bike is its versatility. Unlike some of the motorized monstrosities designed as all-terrain vehicles, it can be used out on the road without discomfort or embarrassment. It makes a fine commuting machine, although if you have a long commute, you may be better off with a bike that's faster on the road.

COMBINATION BIKES: ROAD BIKES AND HYBRIDS

Most bikes combine the characteristics of two of these three basic types of bikes, and your first bike definitely *should.* When you combine a racing bike and a touring model, you get a *road bike.* An entry-level road bike costs about $350. Mid-priced mountain bikes, priced from about $225 to $600, are more suitable for the road than their exotic, higher-priced counterparts.

A combination road bike and mountain bike, called a hybrid, also exists. I think hybrids are too much of a compromise, though, and don't recommend them. The blended extremes don't tend to work harmoniously. As I said before, most bikes are compromises. They have to be, because they serve more than one purpose and because their versatility attracts buyers. But merging extremes, as in the case of the hybrid, seldom works—if your spouse wants to live in the country, but you prefer the city, moving to the suburbs makes no one happy. Besides, I

Trek calls this model the MultiTrack; most people call it a hybrid or cross-trainer, the common generic terms. Such bikes are necessarily compromises in design, but they're suitable for road and trail, or anything from casual riding to touring. They're priced from less than $300 to about $1,000.

can't really imagine a Jeep that rides smoothly and comfortably on the highway—or corners and accelerates like a sports car.

A road bike, on the other hand, is a happy, sensible compromise that serves most riders very well. It's a practical, almost-all-purpose combination.

TANDEM BIKES

How could a blind man enter the Tour de France, the most prestigious bicycle race in the world? As the stoker (back rider) on a tandem, of course. (Ray Patterson, a blind rider, actually competed in the Tour de France tandem race from 1985 to 1988.)

The tandem bike, or "bicycle built for two," was introduced in the nineteenth century, and has had several periods of minor popularity since then. If you don't count the custom-built oddities used by circus performers and other trick exhibition riders, the tandem is just about the ultimate in specialty bikes. A tandem is undeniably fun for rides with a dependable partner (though in view of the high divorce rate, it may be a risky long-term investment). However, it's long and unwieldy, and may be impractical—or even unsafe—for use in typical traffic situations.

One of the authors owns a specimen, a Western Flyer, made in the 1960s, and it's typical. It has two seats, two sets of pedals, two chains, and two handlebars, but of course only the front handlebar turns. The brakes are on the front handlebars. The forward chain's rear sprocket is between the rear pedals, next to the rear chain's front sprocket. Either chain will turn the rear wheel, and when both riders pedal, the two chains together exert considerable drive power. While tandems can zoom on a flat or downhill,

Like single-seat bicycles, tandems have become somewhat specialized, tailored to the favorite or primary activities of the owners. Here's one designed and built for moderate trail riding. (Photo courtesy of Burley Design Cooperative.)

This tandem is the old Western Flyer described in the text. The crank arms are slightly out-of-phase, perhaps making it easier to start riding. Note also the single front caliper brake, used in conjunction with the rear coaster brake.

they're slow uphill—the bike's and riders' combined weight overshadows the added power.

You can buy tandem frames made for the road or trail. These are serious bikes, not to be confused with the "boardwalk cruisers" rented during the family vacation, or the department-store variety. A tandem's 21 gear combinations are controlled by the "captain," or front rider, and so are the brakes. Every component that plays a part in supporting both riders is made beefier than on a "regular" bike. The wheels can have as many as 48 spokes. Mechanically efficient cantilever brakes, usually used on mountain bikes and some touring models, are standard on tandems, and some even sport drum or disk brakes in the rear.

Tandem frames are available in a mix of sizes, and can accommodate front and rear riders of different sizes. At least one manufacturer, Burley

Design Cooperative, offers a suspension for the stoker; the captain no longer has to warn of approaching bumps!

FOLDING BIKES

During World War II, select groups of U.S. Army Paratroopers were issued experimental two-piece bicycles that came apart at the seat tube. Their construction was simple and ingenious, though hardly new even at that time. (Military services had used bicycles of many kinds for messenger service in World War I, and the Italian, French, and Austrian armies had experimented with folding models even before the turn of the century.) The frame configuration of the Paratroop version was that of the old-fashioned "girl's bike"—a bike without a top tube. Slanting down and rearward from the top of the front fork, the single thick, high-strength tube of the frame fit snugly into a short but very strong locking sleeve between the pedals. This experimental bicycle never saw much service; it was too heavy to be practical for Paratroop use.

Today's folding bikes are just as strong but much lighter. A folding bike can neatly solve a storage-space problem. These marvels of convenience won't win you any races, but they're practical for apartment dwellers or commuters. They literally fold in half, usually hinging or coming apart at the seat tube. Their availability is limited, so you may have to resort to mail order. Check bicycle magazines for ads, or ask a local bike shop or club if they can help in locating one. Ride before you buy if possible, and know the return policy.

Now that we know the bikes, let's look at the assemblies that make up these versatile machines.

THE FRAME

When choosing a bike, put your emphasis on the frame rather than on optional features or accessories—you can add those later. A well-made frame will give you years of quality service, long after all the other components have been replaced several times. It's more than just a few pipes welded together—it bequeaths to the bike the individual personality and character the designer visualized when he specified the

This ingenious machine may look strange, but it's a fairly typical compact "folder," featuring 20-inch wheels. It's pictured with seat and handlebar raised in riding position and folded with seat and handlebar lowered. A collapsible bicycle like this can easily be stored in a small closet.

Here's a folding bicycle made by Dahon, shown ready to go and folded for storage or vehicular transportation. It's a versatile design, employing full-sized 26-inch wheels, like a mountain bike.

dimensions and materials. It gives the bike its true identity. No matter what else is changed, you can't change the basic identity inherent in the design of the frame.

The frame is the bike. Ask it to do something for which it wasn't designed and the frame protests, letting you know something is wrong, yet makes the best of the situation. However, it won't just go along for the ride, which is why it's important to know what kind of frame to buy when you pursue specialized areas of cycling.

Structurally, the frame is to the bike what the I-beam is to a building, and what your skeleton is to you. Everything attached to the bike is attached to the frame. Its job is to support you and to ensure that the back wheel receives the energy you exert pedaling.

Steel alloy is the most popular material for making quality bicycle frames. An alloy is a mixture of two or more metals, and you'll encounter alloy names like high-carbon steel, chromium-molybdenum (cro-moly, for short) and manganese-molybdenum. For a given weight, these alloys and others can be made stronger and stiffer than 100 percent steel. Aluminum, lighter than steel alloy, is readily available today in $500 bikes.

Materials considered more exotic than these "mundane" metals emerge as the latest and greatest in frame technology. Titanium (or titanium alloy) is another metal used. Carbon fiber and other composites are bonded together to fabricate the latest playthings in the quest for zero weight and maximum energy transfer and comfort. Presently, these latest materials are also the most expensive.

All these materials work for bicycle frames and forks, although steel-alloy traditionalists debate the durability and worth of the new technologies. Time will tell, but so far the high-tech materials have succeeded. Millions of miles have been logged on many sorts of materials. People used to ride "centuries" (100-mile rides) in the 1800s. Before the turn of the century, people were attempting transcontinental tours, and at least one completed a "round-the-world" tour. Their bikes didn't weigh less than 25 pounds and had aluminum wheels with high-pressure pneumatic tires!

Advancements in technology are interesting, and some day chemists and metallurgists will develop a material suitable for bicycle frames weighing less than 1 pound and durable enough to withstand a sledgehammer or plastic explosives. But who really needs such frame materials? Unless you plan on doing some pretty competitive cycling—

where your success is measured in hundredths of seconds—buy the bike in your price range that fits and feels best. After all, what does chromium-molybdenum really mean to you, anyway?

I extend this advice to those planning to spend megabucks on a bicycle. If you're in the market for the latest advancements in frame design with the most technologically advanced materials, there are enough exotica out there to keep you interested. If you're really going to spend a thousand dollars or more for a bike, you want to know as much about it as you can, and you may care whether it's made of aluminum or titanium. But your best bet is to go out and ride the thing. Steel alloys are still used in the Tour de France, and one trip to a velodrome will show you that the pros don't all ride the same type of bike.

WHEELS AND TIRES

The bike wheel is assembled from a rim, spokes, and a hub. The rim is made of steel or aluminum alloy. When we speak of an aluminum or steel wheel, it's the rim's material we're talking about. Aluminum wheels are lighter, but, because they're built better, they're also more durable and stay true (round and straight) longer. For any serious riding, and especially if you're going to compete, aluminum wheels are strongly recommended.

Spokes can be single- or double-butted, round or bladed. A double-butted spoke is thinner in the middle than on the ends, to reduce weight. Its beefier ends handle stress better; the end is where most spokes break. Bladed spokes are flat and, hence, more aerodynamic than round spokes, but they're not as strong. You usually see bladed spokes only on the front wheel, which has less stress to deal with.

A wheel is more than the sum of its parts. You can bend a spoke easier than a wire coat hanger. Damaging a rim requires more effort, but don't trust it to a curious toddler. Build the spokes and rim into a wheel, however, and they become surprisingly rugged—they'll take jolts head on without a whimper. (But a slight knock on the side can hurt them; there's no supporting structure on the sides.) If you dare, think about the single spoke and fragile rim the next time you're barrelling down a hill at forty miles per hour—then you'll appreciate the wheel's construction.

Reducing your wheels' weight is the second easiest way to make your bike faster. Reducing *your* weight is the easiest. The wheels are what you must set in motion. And a wheel that's easier to start is easier to stop. (An object in motion tends to stay in motion and all that Isaac Newton stuff.) A light wheel is especially valuable when the rim is wet—a wet aluminum rim stops far quicker than a wet steel rim does.

A wheel is useless without a tire. Both are available in a variety of diameters and widths, so if you're not sure what size tire fits your rim, ask at a bike shop. To get the most from your bike and your wallet, ask also what range of tires will benefit your bike and riding style. Remember, you won't put racing slicks on an economy-priced "utility bike."

Choose a tire based on the kind of bike you have and the type of riding you intend to do. For instance, a 26-inch tire will fit your mountain-bike wheel, but do you want one that's designed for commuting or powering through mud?

Consider the tread when choosing your mountain bike's tire. The tread's purpose is to put as much of the tire in contact with the road

A component's model and style generally reveal the type and/or quality of the bicycle. The small cage on this derailleur indicates that it's used for a small range of gears, appropriate for this racing bike.

surface as possible. The more rubber that contacts the ground, the more control you'll have. Some mountain-bike tires' nodules and spikes are aligned and twisted to have the maximum effect in soft dirt, while others are designed for solid trails. And some are most effective on hard streets. Buy the tires to match the riding you usually do.

A road bike's tire differs here. It may not have a tread. While it's probable that someone has studied the effect of a road-bike tire's tread on wet and dry surfaces, and perhaps even compared its performance on blacktop and concrete, the differences are academic. I've ridden many tread types during tours, races, and just riding around, in cold weather and hot, wet and dry. I never knew what tread was between the road and me.

Tires range in price from about $6 up. You can buy a $6 tire at KMart and it will perform like a $6 tire. Bike shops have loads of splendid $40 tires, but do you need a $40 tire? Buy the tire to match the type of riding you intend to do. For a road bike, something in the mid-price range will serve most riders admirably.

DERAILLEURS AND GEARS

Change gears by moving a shift lever or rotating a ring next to a handgrip. Most road bikes have two levers mounted on the downtube (the frame tube that slopes at a 45-degree angle from the front of the bike to the bottom center), although some less expensive models mount the levers on the handlebar stem. It may look awkward, but reaching the downtube-mounted levers is more natural—your hand lands at the levers as your arm drops from the handlebar. Touring bikes frequently have levers stuck in the handlebar ends. On the latest road-bike system (available on $1000+ racers or as $350 accessories) you nudge a brake lever sideways to shift gears. A mountain bike has its shifting control mounted to the handlebar, so it can be flicked with the thumb, or next to the handgrip, and is easily rotated. Both mountain-bike systems permit shifting without removing your hands from the handlebars.

When you flick or rotate the control, a derailleur moves. The derailleur and the lever are attached by a cable. The derailleur's job is twofold: it moves the chain from cog to cog, and it takes up slack in the chain. Your bike probably has two derailleurs—one in the front and one in the rear.

Derailleurs for mountain bikes and road bikes differ mainly in their cage length. The cage is the part of the derailleur through which the chain passes. A wider gear range requires a longer or wider cage. So, mountain bikes and touring bikes have longer rear cages and wider front cages than racing bikes have. A racer's derailleur cages are shorter and narrower and so permit crisper shifts. Narrower gear ranges require less "extra" chain, so a smaller, lighter cage can be used.

About ten years ago, index shifting (also called "click" shifting, because of the sound it makes) appeared. When you move an indexed shifter, it stops at the next detent, so you move it from one "notch" to another, and it "clicks." You can't miss. To shift gears, simply flick or rotate to the next detent as you pedal.

As you read the discussion of gearing, it will be helpful to refer to this diagram of the drivetrain, showing the various components from the front assembly to the rear assembly.

Before index shifting, you moved the lever until the pedaling resistance changed and you heard the chain jump. Then you "fine tuned" it until the rattling stopped. It wasn't difficult—you quickly got used to how far you had to move the lever.

The difference between indexed and non-indexed shifting always reminded me of the fingering difference between a guitar and a violin. The indexed shifting has detents to stop the lever from moving. A guitar has frets to guide you, so your finger position doesn't have to be as precise. Both instruments are capable of producing beautiful music, though. I still use the non-indexed shifting on my touring bike, which is about fourteen years old.

Before bikes were chain-driven, the distance a bike could travel with one pedal revolution was determined by the size of the front wheel—the first pedaled bikes were "front-wheel drive," like today's children's tricycles. It was impractical to carry extra front wheels (of different diameters), so the chain-driven bike was developed, then improved by equipping it with gears that you could change by flicking a lever. But mechanical complexity may lead to mis-understanding, so let's see if we can clarify this sometimes perplexing issue of gears.

For any gear combination, you can easily figure out how far one pedal revolution will take you. Then you can determine what gear to shift to next because your present gear is no longer adequate.

Determine how far one pedal revolution will take you by dividing the number of teeth on any front sprocket by the number of teeth on any rear sprocket. This quotient, multiplied by the diameter of your rear wheel, is the gear inches *for that gear combination only.* Gear inches multiplied by pi (3.14) will tell you how far you'll travel with one revolution of the pedals—again, for that gear combination.

Let's back up for a second. If you figure out the gear-inch number for each combination, you can construct a chart to show you what the orderly sequence of your gears is. Then you can systematically decide what gear to shift to next when the pedaling gets too easy or too hard. You'll also see how the gears for a racing bike differ from those on a touring bike or mountain bike.

Let's assume I have a bike that has two front sprockets, one with 42 teeth and one with 52 teeth, and a 700C (or 27-inch) wheel. On the back wheel of my bike are 6 sprockets; one sprocket with 13 teeth, another with 15, the next with 17, then 20, then 24, and the largest with 28. With these figures I can construct a chart that looks like this:

	42	52
13		
15		
17		
20		
24		
28		

Now fill in the blanks using the formula for gear inches I described above. (Use a diameter of 27 inches for a 700C wheel.) The chart will look like this:

	42	52
13	87	108
15	76	94
17	67	83
20	57	70
24	47	59
28	41	50

The numbers in the boxes are the gear inches. The lowest of those is first gear; the highest is twelfth. You can see how their order jumps back and forth between the 42-tooth front sprocket and the 52-tooth front sprocket. The steps increase in this order; 42/28, 42/24, 52/28, 42/20, 52/24, 42/17, 52/20, 42/15, 52/17, 42/13, 52/15, 52/13. But you need to simplify that progression, because you should avoid using any gear combination that would result in too much chain deflection. Therefore, you can delete 42/13 and 52/28. And looking closely at the gear inches, you can see that 42/20 and 52/24 are very close. So let's drop the 52/24 (there's more chain deflection, and experience will teach you it's less practical to shift into). Finally, the 42/15 seems like a logical step but is too impractical to get to, so we'll forget about that. Four gear combinations are impractical—our marketed 12-speed has been reduced to a useable eight-speed.

But the next problem is, how do you use this knowledge when you're pedaling along. An experienced, skillful cyclist can glance down and see the position of the chain on one or another front and rear sprocket. Being familiar with the chart I've given for gear combinations (or a similar chart for his bike's gearing), he can see if the front/rear combination is a good one. In fact, he'll, know what gear he's in by the feel of the pedals or by unconsciously "counting."

The average rider doesn't remember the chart in that manner, but it's useful simply as a reminder that not all gear combinations will increase efficiency. For the average rider, the rule is to let your legs tell you when to shift—and whether to go up or down one *more* position.

On some of the new mountain bikes and hybrids the gears are numbered right at the shifting mechanism on the handlebar, so you can actually see what gear combination you choose. For most cyclists, however, the procedure remains to shift by feel, aided by knowledge of the various charted combinations.

The gearing chart used as an example was for a typical road bike. If you create a similar chart for a touring bike and a mountain bike, you'll see that those two are very similar. The mountain bike will have more usable low gears for climbing steep dirt hills, and the touring bike will have more usable gears in the middle and top range, which is more practical for the road.

Racing bikes, on the other hand, will have a very narrow range, so the rider can choose more precisely the gear he needs to maintain the cadence with which he's most comfortable. (Remember, that's why you shift gears—to maintain the cadence at which you're most efficient.) For this reason, too, it makes more sense to call gears by their combination, instead of saying first gear or fifth gear. Fifth gear on the mountain bike is in a different position from fifth gear on the racer. And fifth gear on one mountain bike may be different from fifth gear on another mountain bike.

The best gear spacing will always be arguable, but I must commend some bike manufacturers and lash out at others for their gear selections. Too often I see high gears of 108 inches (52/13), and even higher, being stepped from a 94-inch gear (52/15). Not only is 108 inches an awfully big gear, but it's a big jump from a 94. These are on entry-level and mid-priced bikes. Many of us would need thighs like tree trunks and steel knees to push a gear that big. Why not be sensible and bring back the 52/14 as the high gear? It would get far more use and would be a more logical step from the next lower gear. Some manufacturers have already begun.

When you're considering a specialty bike, or any bike from a good bike shop, don't overlook the gears. If the gear combination is impractical for you, ask your dealer to change it—many will do this for nothing when you buy the bike.

BRAKES

Brakes generally come in two forms today—sidepull and centerpull. Two calipers form the brake, and sidepulls are so named because the cable that activates them pulls the caliper from the side. They're more precise in their movements and mechanically simpler, so you get a better feel as you're stopping. Road bikes are usually equipped with sidepull brakes, although bikes designed for heavy touring and trail riding often have a modern form of centerpull called the cantilever.

Centerpull brakes are advantageous when higher leverage is required or desired, as on mountain bikes navigating steep, loose trails, or touring bikes loaded with an extra 25 pounds of gear. You'd think cantilever brakes could stop a truck. One cable attaches to two arms which pivot on their own posts. Since they're a little more complex than other brakes, you have to move the brake lever a little farther to move the brake pads to the rim—but not much. Actually, you want that bit of "free play." A mountain bike's fat, low-pressure tires prevent you from feeling the road as well as you can on a racing bike whose narrow tires are inflated to 120 psi.

Good brakes feel firm, no matter how hard you squeeze. Lesser brakes "mush" as you squeeze harder—it feels like the brake pad is compressing, or that you're squeezing through stiff mashed potatoes. Also, stopping power comes from your hand squeezing the brake lever and thus squeezing the brake shoe against the rim. Therefore, flexing a caliper wastes energy.

BOTTOM BRACKET
AND HEADSET

Two less prominent components, but obviously necessary, are the bottom bracket and the headset. The bottom bracket is the bearing assembly on which the pedal crank turns. The headset is the assembly on which the front fork and handlebar stem turn, thus permitting the bike to be steered.

SELECTING A USED BIKE

Bargains can be found in used bikes—if you know what you're looking for. People usually sell bikes for one of two opposite reasons. They either use a bike often, and now want to upgrade, or they never use it at all.

Familiarize yourself with what's on the market through magazine articles and advertisements, bike-shop displays, manufacturers' brochures, and equipment catalogs. Get to know what components are standard on ATBs and on road bikes, and get to know which are the top of the line and which are middle of the road. For example, as this book goes to print, Shimano offers several component series, called the 105, 600, Ultegra, and Dura-Ace. The Dura-Ace is their top of the line, well respected throughout the bicycle industry, and even used by some racing pros in the Tour de France and other prestigious races where an equipment malfunction eliminates you. The 105, while still a very respectable line, is far less expensive than the Dura-Ace, and it's good enough to accommodate all but the most demanding amateurs.

Lesser components, such as those offered on entry-level bikes, are seldom offered in parts catalogs, and here a quick trip to a bike shop to look at the less expensive bikes will tell you what's what.

Components can give you a clue as to what level of bike you're looking at, but, as with a new bike, it's the frame you're most interested in. Know how to spot a quality, undamaged frame, or get a knowledgeable friend involved.

Check the frame scrupulously, using your common sense to guide your appraisal. Are there any tiny cracks in the welds where the tubes are joined? Are there any bent tubes, or other evidence of a crash? Is there any rust? Does the fork look damaged or misaligned?

Move to the wheels. Are there any broken spokes? Do they spin true (without wobble)? Is there any other evidence of incoherency?

Try the brakes before you ride the bike. Slowly squeeze the levers and make sure the brake pads contact the rim at about the same time.

Make sure the bike is your size and fits you acceptably. (See Chapter 2 for fitting the bike to you.) It's common to buy a used bike that doesn't fit perfectly, but it shouldn't be so ill-fitting as to be dangerous. You must be able to straddle the bike without the top tube hitting your crotch. You should

A bona fide bicycle shop, like Genesis Bicycles in Easton, Pennsylvania, sells higher-quality bikes and carries a wider selection than a department store. Such a shop also stocks a truly complete array of accessories. The sales staff is knowledgeable and will guide the customer in selecting an appropriate bike, adjusting it for proper fit, and choosing related gear wisely. You may pay a higher price for all this, but it's more than worth the cost for riding beyond your neighborhood.

be able to reach for the handlebars without feeling uncomfortably extended. The brake levers shouldn't be so large that your fingers won't reach around them (although you can have smaller levers installed), a common complaint from people with small hands.

Shopping for a used bike isn't a whole lot different from buying a used car (though it is a whole lot simpler). The seller should be willing to let you take a short test drive.

Begin riding slowly, getting a feel for the bike. Test the brakes before you gain too much speed. As you gain confidence in the bike, concentrate on how it feels as a whole, noting the steering and predictability.

Buying a used bike can be a means of getting a better bicycle than a new one costing the same money. But remember, the frame is the bike, and repairing a broken frame is unreliably risky at best. Safety is essential, and you certainly don't want to put all the money you saved into the purchase of replacement parts.

TIPS ON RENTING BIKES

You can rent a bike, but how safe, dependable, and enjoyable it will be may depend on where you rent it and how carefully you examine it. Unfortunately, the selection tends to be rather limited, and often so is the quality. It's rarely cost-efficient in the long run. Since you're reading this book, I presume your interest in cycling is more than casual.

Some years ago, one of the authors rented a bike on three separate occasions from a New York City bike shop. The first was rented while he was having his own bike professionally repaired. (He loved his somewhat battered old bike and wasn't yet ready to part with it and buy a new one.) The second occasion was after his bike had been stolen and he was making a month-long project out of shopping for a new one. The third was for a bikeless friend who wanted to accompany him on an overnight trip.

All three rentals were happy experiences. That is, the bikes fit well enough (with minor adjustments) and performed well enough. That, surely, was largely because the bicycles were rented from a bike shop whose knowledgeable owner was interested not only in repeat business but in turning renters into buyers. The machines the shop kept on hand for rental were used (actually, very used) but of reasonably good quality, and the proprietor took pains to keep them in good condition.

You may be able to find a local bike shop where reasonably good rental bicycles are available, but not every bike shop counts on that kind of business, and other rental outlets tend to be less reliable than those specializing in bicycles.

Shops that rent furniture and televisions and washers and stereo systems often rent out bikes, too. I'm not talking about the bikes you rent at the beach, which tend to be awful, but the bikes rented elsewhere are generally of the department-store variety and may disappoint you. However, if your sole purpose is just to dabble in cycling, this may be the avenue to take, at least temporarily.

Use the same criteria to choose a rental bike as when picking a used bike, if you have a choice. Always, always, always, check the brakes, wheels, tires, and integrity of the frame before riding a bike you don't know who rode last. Not everyone is considerate enough to report a problem, nor are the rental-shop employees always skilled or interested enough to recognize and fix a problem. And wear a helmet. You should be using one even when you ride your own very dependable bike. With an unfamiliar bike it can be even more important. In some states, the law requires you to wear one.

2

Bike Fit

It's not a good idea to walk into a bike shop, point to the cool purple bike with green accents, announce confidently, "I want that one, please," pay the cashier, and ride off. Choosing a bike is more like buying clothing—you try it on first unless mail order is the only way to get what you want.

Making the bike and you compatible is the most important part of choosing one, whether it's your first or fourth, new or used. The world's most beautiful suit is useless if it doesn't fit you. As with suits, you first choose your size, then make alterations or adjustments to fit you.

A properly fitted bike quickly feels fluid and natural. No part of the bike stands out. Cycling is like swinging a golf club or tennis racket identically the last thousand times; or driving your car for perhaps the ten thousandth time. You only feel it as a whole. It is synergy imagined.

On the other hand, an ill-fitting frame can make you uncomfortable and inefficient. It might even cause you to have poor control of the bike and end up hospitalized, or worse. Remember those childhood images of the little kid whose bike was so big he had to tilt the seat's nose forward just so his toes barely touched the pedals at the bottom of their strokes? Let's bury that epitome of foolishness. Or have you ever worn clothing that's a size too small while sitting for four hours in the back seat of a subcompact car, then balancing atop a barstool with no footrest for another three hours? Riding an ill-fitting bike is similar.

The almost universal perception that cycling in an upright position is more comfortable, safer, more stable, and better for your back than riding in a bent-over "racing" position needs clarification. If you're casually riding around the neighborhood for thirty minutes three nights a week, you could probably ride as though you were riding an old Harley, leaning back with

31

your hands clasped behind your head, and never notice the difference. For longer rides, though, the bent-over position has tremendous advantages.

Racers and distance riders use this bent-over position because it's more efficient and more comfortable for their purposes. ATB riders on the trail demand a more upright (though not as upright as the hybrid rider) position because it's more beneficial to trail riding—*their* purpose.

The most critical dimensions in fitting you to the bike have to do with the contact points. These are the points at which body and bike touch—hands and handlebars, feet and pedals, seat and seat. We'll refer to these points again when discussing clothing for cycling.

Look at the accompanying illustration. The three contact points naturally comprise two lines. Line A/B, known as the seat tube, determines the frame size. When the salesperson says you need an 18-inch frame, it's the length of this tube he's talking about. As you can see, the frame size you need is largely determined by your leg length. (This mustn't be confused with the wheel size. Wheel size is the diameter of the wheel; it has nothing to do with the frame.)

Your torso length will be accounted for by the length of the top tube (line A/C) in conjunction with the length of the stem (the component your handlebars slip into).

On a quality frame, the seat tube and top tube will "grow" as the frame

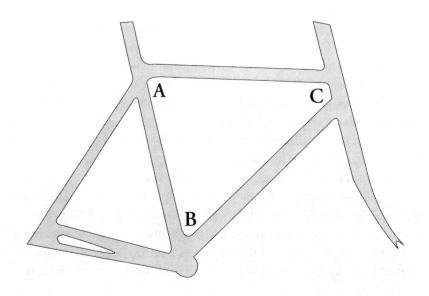

gets bigger to accommodate taller riders. In other words, a taller rider with longer legs will also have a longer torso, so the frame is built longer as well as taller. Less expensive frames will come in taller sizes, but probably not longer. Department-store bikes usually come in two sizes—men's and women's. The women's model is smaller but the same length and may or may not have a top tube. A bike with a frame that's proportioned for length as well as height—in a sense, "customized"—costs more, but is worth it.

For women, a frame designed specifically to meet their physical proportions has appeared in recent years. This frame style differs from the outdated top-tubeless "girl's bike." The women's models I'm talking about are real bikes with frames to rival their male counterparts. Even if you're a man, it's worthwhile to audition these bikes if you're considerably smaller than average or having difficulty finding a frame on which you feel comfortable.

Earlier, we referred to different tube lengths, which govern the way the bike "wears" you. Now we'll look harder at the frame, at the angles and details that make it behave and feel the way it does, and why certain dimensions are effective for mountain bikes and touring bikes but not for racers, and vice versa.

UNDERSTANDING FRAME DIMENSIONS

Familiarize yourself with the accompanying illustration. All bikes have approximately this shape. Granted, some of the mountain bikes look so exotic you'd think they were designed for roving the moon—and I'll bet some of them could—but they still have the same basic configuration.

Here are the elements of configuration whose angles or lengths influence a bike's character and capabilities.

HTA (head-tube angle)—The steeper this angle is, the quicker your bike will turn.

STA (seat-tube angle)—Increasing this angle puts you in a more forward, "sprinty," less relaxed position.

ChSt (chain stay length)—Increasing this length makes the bike more stable, with a softer feel.

BB (bottom bracket height)—Increasing this height allows more ground and cornering clearance.

WhBs (wheelbase length)—Increasing the wheelbase length makes the bike more stable.

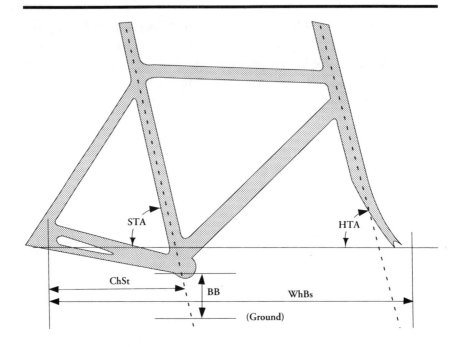

Now, compare some typical frame dimensions of stock mountain bikes, touring bikes, and racing bikes. Angles are in degrees; lengths are in inches.

Typical Bike Dimensions

	ATB	Touring	Racing
Seat-tube Angle	73.5°	73.5°	73°
Head-tube Angle	71°	72.3°	73°
Chainstay Length	17"	18"	16"
Bottom Bracket Height	11.6"	10.4"	10.8"
Wheelbase	43"	41.6"	38.5"

When you compare these dimensions, some noticeable—and predictable—things appear. The racing bike likes to be more responsive, and its rider had better not expect the cushy ride he'll find on one of the other two machines. On the other hand, the racing bike feels more solid because there's less frame flex.

The ATB is clearly designed for stability, and requires it. When you're creeping over a trail with rocks jutting here and there, stability can become a premium.

The touring bike is designed for comfort. Its long chainstays soak up imperfections in the road.

Now that you know what the numbers say, let's look closely at each bike.

Seat adjustments. You'll recall my mentioning that ATBs are longer and lower-framed than road bikes. This means the two types won't—or shouldn't—fit you the same way if you're to achieve maximum, energy-efficient comfort and the high degree of control needed for maximum safety. Straddling a mountain-bike frame in stockinged feet should allow you a 3- to 5-inch clearance between your crotch and the top tube. One inch of clearance for a road bike is right.

Next, let's fine-tune the bike's measurements to your requirements. Have someone hold the bike while you sit on it as though you were

SADDLE

SEAT CLAMP

SEAT POST

SEAT TUBE QUICK RELEASE

REAR BRAKE

FREEWHEEL

HANDLEBAR STEM

BRAZE-ON
(for water bottle cage)

FRONT DERAILLEUR

CHAINRING

CRANK

HANDLEBAR

BRAKE LEVER

HEADSET

FRONT BREAK CABLE

FRONT CANTILEVER BRAKE

FORK

TIRE

RIM

DERAILLEUR CABLE

REAR DERAILLEUR

DERAILLEUR CAGE

CHAIN

BOTTOM BRACKET

TOE STRAP

PEDAL

TOE CLIP

QUICK RELEASE SKEWER

SPOKE

HUBSET

Jennifer Jones demonstrates the straddle test, the first step to perform when checking a bike's fit. A road bike should allow one inch of clearance between your crotch and the top tube. A mountain bike's tube should clear by three to five inches.

riding. Wearing the same shoes you'll be riding in, place your heels on the pedals and pedal slowly backward. Adjust the seat height so your knee is slightly bent when your feet reach the bottom of the circle, but not so high that you're rocking back and forth in the saddle.

To check for proper extension of your torso, stay in the riding position. For mountain bikes, your back should be straight and your arms bent comfortably while you're leaning forward about 45 degrees.

Advice for road bikes is a bit more specific. A plumb line dropped from the tip of your nose should land in the center of the handlebars. The handlebars should eclipse the front hub when you lower your eyes. Your arms should be slightly bent, and you should be leaning forward while keeping your back straight.

You can raise or lower the seat to get the proper leg extension. But if you're too cramped or too stretched out along the top tube, you must change the stem. Ask your bike shop to help you with this. There are limits to how far you can go in length without the danger of breaking the stem, surely an incident you'll want to avoid when flying down a hill at 50 miles per hour or picking your way through trees and poison ivy on a trail.

These are the most critical adjustments you must make when setting up your bike, but you may as well set up the following refinements, also. They'll add much to your riding enjoyment.

Saddle tilt. ATB riders can experiment; pointing the saddle's nose up reduces arm strain, but pointing it down lowers chances of irritation. Any deviation from level should be slight. Road-bike riders should keep the saddle level, although some women prefer a slight tilt downward.

Seat fore/aft. With the pedals horizontal, a plumb line dropped from the front of your knee should bisect the pedal's axis. This is the same for mountain and road bikes.

The author shows how the road-racing bike "wears the rider" differently from the mountain bike. The two types of machine are designed for very different kinds of riding. Proper riding positions can be compared to driving positions in certain cars. A true sports car has the rider sitting low and stretched out for optimal racing efficiency, while a Jeep has the driver sitting up straighter.

Toe clips. Properly sized toe clips will allow the ball of your foot to be positioned over the pedal spindle. Don't assume that just because a bike comes equipped with toe clips, they're the right size for you. Foot size isn't always proportional to leg length, so you may need to get larger or smaller toe clips.

When you leave the bike shop with your new bike, they will have set it up to fit you. You were a part of the process. They'll have asked you to straddle the bike and mount as we described before. They'll have asked you to place your heels on the pedals and pedal backward, so they can see how high to put the seat. Cooperate with them; ask questions and request explanations of anything you don't understand. It's your money, and your safety.

One of the reasons you chose for going to a bike shop (even if a local department store has a better than usual selection of bicycles) is the knowledge and expert help provided by the salesperson. He'll help you get the most out of your bike by setting it up properly for you.

Toe clips greatly improve your riding efficiency. They're available in different sizes, so make sure your clips position the ball of your foot over the pedal spindle, as shown here.

You can ride your new bike now. Pay attention to how the bike feels, what feels right and what feels awkward. If you're a rekindled rider, you may be amazed at how efficient today's bikes feel compared to the English racers of twenty years ago. When all the adjustments work right, the bike will feel as though it's an extension of your body and limbs.

Most likely, you'll want to fine-tune the bike to suit your preferences. Abide by the rules we spoke of above, and make adjustments no more than one centimeter at a time. Eventually you'll get to the point where you realize you've gone too far. This is why it's essential to familiarize yourself with the setup procedure we talked about above.

Tinkering with your setup is healthy, but know how to put it back where you started, especially if you discover you need to make an adjustment fifteen miles from home.

3

Accessories

There are tons of accessories you can get for cycling—some necessary or useful, many useless, many fashionable, and a few downright dangerous. I won't tell you what you don't need but can safely add; if something will encourage you to ride or you simply think it might be fun, then get it. I will tell you the necessities, and what's dangerous. I won't dwell on what's fashionable.

When I say necessities, I really mean accessories you should get before all others. If you buy everything at the same time you buy your bike, you'll spend an additional hundred dollars, not always an easy cost to absorb. So let's start with what you absolutely need.

HELMETS

I'm often asked if helmets work. The answer is a resounding *yes*—they absorb the impact destined for your head and spread it out before it can get to your skull, distributing the impact over a larger area. Some states require helmets for minors only or for all cyclist.

Helmets come in all sorts of styles, colors, sizes, weights, and brands. Many are so light and comfortable that you forget you're wearing one, and all have cooling vents so you don't roast. Most helmets are made of expanded polystyrene foam covered with a strong plastic shell. New materials have come out, but they all seem to work on the same principle.

Unfortunately, there's no universal standard with which to compare one helmet to another, so we settle for something approved by SNELL, ANSI, and/or ASTM. These are organizations that set up standards they feel helmets should meet. If you have a helmet that is SNELL 90, this is not a lifesaving guarantee, but it's certainly reassuring.

Fitting the helmet is of the utmost importance for both safety and comfort, just like the fit of your bike. An ill-fitting helmet won't stay in place when you need it most, and won't be very comfortable when it's merely resting on your head waiting to absorb impact.

If you have an accident while wearing your helmet, let the manufacturer determine whether or not it was damaged, even if it looks okay. One manufacturer, Specialized, makes this statement: "As with any helmet, its ability to absorb the forces generated in the collision may be substantially reduced." Let the experts determine whether your helmet's force-absorbing characteristics have been substantially reduced—don't fool around with your head. Most major manufacturers offer some replacement program for helmets that are worn in an accident.

One final thought: your head weighs about as much as a bowling ball.

Fit your helmet to *your* head by inserting the proper pads that all helmets are supplied with. You'll probably also have to adjust your helmet straps one way for warm-weather cycling and another to accommodate a cap under it for winter riding.

This rider's helmet properly straps under her chin securely, but not too tightly. Remember, it's designed to fit you when you're on your bike, so simulating the riding position while adjusting it will feel different than if you're standing straight.

Imagine dropping a bowling ball from six feet onto concrete. Think of the impact. Now hurl that bowling ball onto the concrete as hard as you can. That could be your head if you're struck by a car or if you crash while barreling down a hill.

GLOVES

Many cyclists use gloves only on cold days. However, there are light, ventilated gloves for warm weather, and they're a good idea. Even light ones offer some protection from bruises, cuts, and abrasions.

I use gloves for safety as well as comfort. They cushion your hands from fatigue, road shock, and the road in case of a fall. They're available

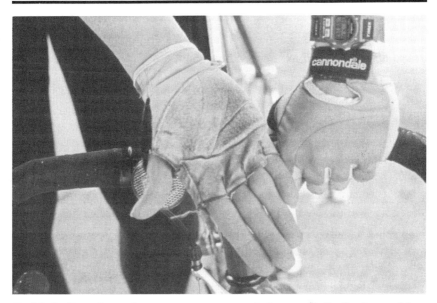

Padded, fingerless gloves are recommended, especially for long rides. These gloves are for warm-weather road cycling. You can also get gloves designed for mountain biking and cold weather.

Al Sagazio, Sr., demonstrates good riding sense by wearing a helmet and gloves. With his hands in one of the recommended five positions on the handlebar, he's also showing good form, which is important in delaying or reducing fatigue.

for both road and trail riding. Otherwise, there's very little to say about these simple but essential items, except that I wouldn't consider taking a ride outside the neighborhood without them.

TOE CLIPS AND STRAPS

Toe clips and straps are indispensable for improving your riding efficiency. Not only do they let you power the bike throughout the pedal stroke (instead of just carrying your foot along on the up pedal stroke); they save you the energy of keeping your foot on the pedal. You'll never want to ride without toe clips once you've become used to them, unless you use the clipless pedal system, which we'll discuss later in this chapter. Toe clips usually come in medium and large sizes—the correct size positions the ball of your foot over the pedal spindle.

Toe clips let you exert force on the pedal throughout its revolution. You'll like them if you've never ridden with them before. You'll get used to them in almost no time, and in an emergency they'll release your feet instantly. An alternative is the clipless pedal system.

Many people think toe clips are unsafe. They fear that they can't get their feet out of the clips in an emergency, or that they'll look foolish when they just fall over at a stoplight. You won't fall over, because you're not locked in; if the toe clips are that tight, you'll cut off the circulation to your toes. Even with cycling shoes, I can slip my foot out of the clip instantly without loosening the strap.

On one occasion, toe clips probably saved me from breaking my ankle or seriously damaging my knee by holding my foot during a fall. I was daydreaming, and tried crossing a wet, open-grate, steel bridge at about 25 miles per hour—much too fast for a steel-grate surface. These bridges are very slippery when wet, and I was sliding across steel before I knew what happened. Luckily, the toe clip held my foot on the pedal. I admit I didn't ride the bike down on purpose, but there's no telling what I would have injured if I had put my foot down while falling at that speed. So toe clips can be a safety device, too.

WATER BOTTLE AND CAGE

It's impractical and dangerous to carry a canteen full of water on your person whenever you venture out on your bike for a rousing ride. So the classic water bottle, clipped to the bike's frame, emerges as a safety device when you consider the dangers of dehydration.

I've never seen a bad cage sold in a bike shop. They're very simple inventions, and if they're strong enough to hold a bottle full of water, they should be strong enough to last at least several seasons. Occasionally they'll break at the welds, although I've never broken one. I carry two, one on my down tube and one on the seat tube.

The water bottle should simply be a plastic bottle with a lid and stopper on it. The bottle should be soft enough so you can squeeze it and squirt liquid through the stopper. Department stores sell insulated bottles, but you don't need that—when your body needs water, it doesn't care whether it's cool or warm water. Insulated bottles are more expensive, and dropping the bottle will break the glass insulation, thus rendering your water supply (and bottle) useless.

Bottles come in 21- and 28-ounce sizes. I prefer the larger size, but make sure your frame is large enough to accommodate it. I prefer the

Water bottles are available in two sizes which fit in the same cage.

It's not always practical (or possible) to reach for your water bottle on a jolting trail. Or, if you're racing, you may not want to come out of your crouched, aerodynamic position or take a hand from your handlebar when you're in the middle of a crowded pack. This back-strapped invention is essentially a canteen with a long, flexible straw, so your hands need never leave the safety of your handlebar and brakes.

bright bottles, but not the clear types. The bright bottles may keep the water slightly cooler in warm weather by reflecting the sunlight, whereas the clear bottles will create a greenhouse effect and heat the water.

MIRROR

A mirror can be a real benefit when cycling in traffic. Glancing into a mirror saves you the trouble of turning your head and possibly drifting into traffic (see Chapter 5). A friend of mine uses a mirror because she can't turn her head far enough to the left without pain.

Some mirrors mount on the handlebars and some on your helmet, but they all let you see behind you without turning your head. Most cyclists prefer the handlebar type, perhaps because they're more similar to a car's side-view mirror.

TOOL KIT AND PUMP

Bikes are machines, and thus susceptible to breakdowns. These breakdowns are most likely to happen when you have no convenient means of correcting them, so the most logical solution is to carry a small tool kit. These tools will add weight, but if you compare the energy you'll expend carrying the tools to the energy and time you'll spend walking your bike home, you'll realize the tools aren't so heavy after all.

Repairing Flats

Probably 99.9 percent of flat tires are due to a hole in the tube or tire. (The other 0.1 percent of flats are due to loose, broken, or missing valve stems.) Covering the hole with a patch is adequate, unless the slice in the tire or tube is larger than the patch, in which case you must replace the tube and cover the slice in the tire with a tire boot (a small piece of rubber cut from an old tire, about an inch long). The boot is to prevent the tube from bulging through the hole in the tire after the tube is pumped up. Such bulging is most prevalent with high-pressure road tires.

A typical tube-repair kit includes sandpaper or scraper, rubber cement, and patches. Instructions are usually included with the patch kit, but here's the general procedure:

To repair a flat, roughen the tube around the puncture and spread a

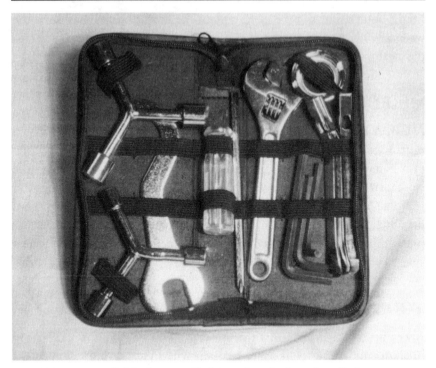

Tool kits are available in neat little packs, designed to fit in your seat pack. They contain everything you need for most minor roadside repairs. But be sure you also have a tube-repair kit.

small amount of rubber cement over and around the hole, slightly larger than the patch. When the rubber cement is thoroughly dry (about three to five minutes), peel the backing off the patch and press the patch over the puncture. To adhere, the patch must contact the rubber cement; you can't stick the patch directly to the tube. (For more information, see Chapter 10.)

After repairing the leak, you can easily replace the lost air with a frame pump. A frame pump mounts to your bike's frame, either to lugs brazed to the frame or with a clamp. If the pump doesn't come with the clamp, a small Velcro strap works perfectly to hold the pump to the top tube—I use one on my touring bike, and they're available at your bike shop.

Several years ago, "canned air" appeared on the market. This is just a small canister of pressurized carbon dioxide, dispensed through a trigger dispenser and capable of inflating a high-pressure tire. Mountain bikes

This rider has patched a hole in his tube, and now he's replacing the air with his frame pump. The modern frame pump, though extremely compact, is very easy, fast, and efficient to use.

may require two cartridges to fill their wider tires. These canisters work, but I prefer the simplicity and reliability of a frame pump.

In all, to fix a flat you need at least two tire levers (to pry the tire from the rim), a tire-repair kit, spare inner tube, tire boot, pump or can of air, and perhaps a pressure gauge. If you have sew-up tires (those tires in which the tire and tube are one "assembly"), you'll need a spare sew-up tire, glue to mount it, and a pumping device. Mountain bikes don't use sew-ups.

Occasionally, you'll want to make a minor adjustment during your ride—perhaps lower the seat or adjust a derailleur. Today you can easily adjust your bike with just a few tools—a set of hex keys, a small (#1) Phillips screwdriver, and a small (1/8") flat-bladed screwdriver. I carry a pocketknife with the screwdrivers folding neatly inside. I prefer the hex keys on a ring, like a key chain. Hex keys are also available in a small

As its name implies, the frame pump fits handily and securely between the frame tubes. Note also the shift lever mounted on the down tube in front of the water bottle, a common arrangement on road bikes.

These are the tools the authors carry for day rides. The top four items are for flat-tire repair. The hex keys are for adjustments. A multi-bladed pocketknife is always useful. The U-shaped tool is a spoke wrench. The coins are for an emergency phone call.

folding tool that looks like a pocketknife, and often has the screwdrivers in with them, but I find this all-in-one tool to be less convenient.

I also carry a spoke wrench to true a wheel knocked out of alignment by a wayward rock, pothole or curb, although I've never had to use it in the middle of a ride. The spoke wrench has a slot that fits over the nipple, the end of the spoke that enters the rim. Turn the nipples around the wobble no more than a sixteenth of a turn at a time until the wobble disappears. Note that the spokes go to opposite sides of the hub, and so adjacent spokes must be turned in opposite directions. See Chapter 10 for more details on truing a wheel.

The whole tool kit contains tire levers, tire-repair kit, spare inner tube, pumping device, hex keys, and Phillips and flat-blade screwdrivers. All except the frame pump will fit inside a mid-sized seat pack, and all are available at bike shops.

BETTER SEAT

Most riders will get a sore butt if they ride long enough. Cycling shorts help, but I recommend upgrading your seat whether or not you get cycling shorts. After-market seats are tailored to fit you and to the specific type of riding you intend to do. Also, men's and women's models support and cushion for the differences in build between the sexes.

Gel seats are excellent. The gel distributes your weight over a larger

After-market parts have been in common use since the 19th century—some of them excellent, others almost laughable. Replacement and upgrade parts of the 1890s included this "Anatomically Perfect" saddle—a very far cry (of discomfort?) from today's easy-riding gel seats.

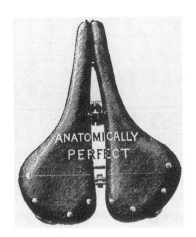

area than just the three pelvic points on which you sit. I use the same gel seat on both my racing and touring bikes.

Leather seats are still available, and some riders swear by them for comfort. The mixed blessing is that it takes time to break one in, but then it conforms to you. After that, this custom-formed seat should last a long time.

SHORTS

Cycling shorts are more than a fashion statement. *Real* cycling shorts are padded, and the pad cushions as well as wicks away moisture. Cycling shorts are shaped to conform to your body in the riding position, have no seams where you sit, and are cut long and hug your leg to prevent chafing. Touring and ATB shorts provide external pockets. Some riders prefer them because they aren't skin-tight—they fit more like walking shorts.

Shorts are made from panels sewn together, the idea being that the more panels there are, the better they'll fit and the more comfortable

Real cycling shorts, available at bike shops but not at many department stores, have a pad in the crotch that not only supplies some cushioning but also wicks away perspiration.

they'll be. It's a viable idea, but try the shorts on before buying. As with any clothing, some brands fit better than others.

SHOES

Every sport has a specialized shoe, and cycling is no different. The cycling shoe's stiff sole provides comfort and efficiency. Additionally, some shoes interlock with the pedal so you can pedal in circles, instead of just pushing down. These include racing shoes and shoes forming a component of the clipless pedal system, both of which will be described below.

Shoes have become more and more specialized over the years to suit specific needs. For simplicity, let's look at them in three basic categories— shoes for road racing, for mountain biking, and for touring. Some are versatile enough to use either on the road or off, but, like the hybrid bikes, they don't excel at either.

For hard, fast, road racing, you need a shoe that doesn't flex, so you

Touring shoes can be used for a variety of cycling activities. They have a stiff sole for riding comfort and efficiency, and they loosely engage with the plate on the pedal. You can easily walk with this type of cycling shoe.

These racing shoes don't flex, so they transmit to the pedal as much energy as you can give. They also interlock with the pedal more securely than touring shoes, and the cleat is adjustable to let you align your foot naturally. Walking is awkward in these shoes, however— hobbling might be a more accurate description. Note how the adjustable cleat interlocks with the plate on the back of the pedal.

push the pedal down and not your heel. Also, these shoes have a cleat that catches with a plate on the pedal. (This isn't to be confused with the clipless pedal system, which has been mentioned before and will be discussed momentarily.) The cleat is often adjustable, so you can align it to the way your foot naturally rests on the pedal. This can prevent knee pain. Because these shoes don't bend, you hobble rather than walk when you wear them. It's not uncommon to see such shoes parked outside stores along with the bikes while their wearers buy supplies.

Riding on the trail offers different challenges than riding on the road. Sometimes you must dismount and carry or push your bike over rugged, unpredictable terrain, so you need a shoe that provides solid, nonslip footing. Also, because the ATB pedal differs from the road pedal, the shoe interfaces differently. A shoe designed for trail riding can be essential if you want to push mountain biking to its limits. These shoes are designed for pedaling, not walking, but they're easier to walk in than stiff-soled road-racing shoes.

If top-notch performance isn't your goal, then consider a shoe made for touring or moderate trail riding. These shoes are comfortable to walk in, but also provide a relatively stiff sole, making cycling easier than with sneakers (which are often hard to get into toe clips). I like the convenience of being able to walk comfortably in my cycling shoes, so I use a touring shoe for all my riding.

The latest boon in cycling shoes is the clipless pedal system. It's available for both ATB and road bikes. The clipless pedal and mated shoe form a great system, although at a higher cost than the standard pedal toe-clip system. The shoe and pedal are interfacing components, like a ski boot and binding.

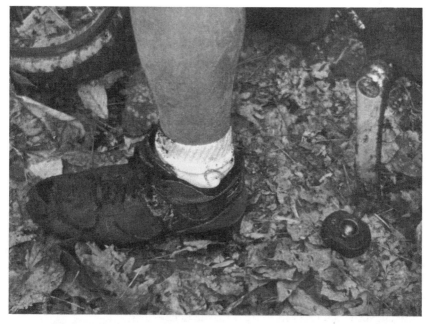

This ATB shoe is easy to walk in and provides good traction if you have to walk your mountain bike. It engages with the clipless pedal visible to the right of the rider's foot.

Top view of the clipless pedal, which directly engages the cyclist's shoe.

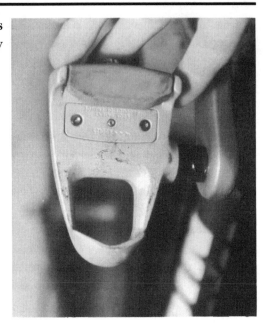

The special cleat and shoe required are now widely available. Indeed, many mid-priced and higher-quality bikes come with clipless pedals as standard equipment. This is a mixed blessing—if you keep that system, you immediately increase the cost of the bike because you must buy compatible shoes, although many bike shops will change components at only the difference in cost. On the other hand, this system does offer the highest level of performance. Like toe clips, shoes that cleat to or interface with the pedal will come away instantly if the need arises, so they don't present a hazard.

SHIRTS

A good cycling shirt will be close-fitting, have three pockets in the back, and be made of a material like polypropylene or Coolmax to wick away moisture and regulate your body temperature. Cut long in the back, they hang down over your shorts and provide a stable container for the banana or whatever you'll carry in those back pockets.

Coolmax (made by Dupont) and polypropylene work impressively. Other materials do the same thing under different brand names. They're great for a ride that starts in the early morning and will last throughout the

A true cycling shirt has three pockets in the back, and one of them makes a convenient container for road food, which won't get squashed there and can be reached quickly.

day, because you don't have the worry of being either too warm or too cool. These materials really do regulate your body temperature and keep you dry at the same time. When I spend the money for a cycling shirt, I make sure it has this characteristic.

Most cycling shirts are short-sleeved, but heavier, long-sleeved shirts are available.

COLD-WEATHER CYCLING

Cycling in cold weather can be tricky, but staying warm isn't hard. You must combat wind-chill, and the faster you ride, the "windier" it gets. If there's a head wind, the chill is even worse.

You stay warm by trapping a layer of air between you and the outside air. The trapped air creates a boundary so the cold air can't get at you. A cat's fur stands up on a cold winter day, away from its body, so it can trap more air. The opposite happens in the summer. Our goose bumps result from our body trying to raise the hair (when we needed hair to keep us warm) to trap air. Down is a good insulator because it traps air so well.

Trapped air keeps you warm, but the insulator must also allow moisture to escape. Moisture will draw heat from your body quickly— that's how a summer swim cools you. It's uncomfortable being cold, but being cold and damp is miserable.

For cycling, the trick is to trap air and wick moisture away with a minimum amount of bulk. You'd be darned uncomfortable donning your winter jacket and going out for a ride. The answer is layering. Put a good

When you see good cycling togs laid out flat, as they come from the store, the shirt and the shorts look "wrong"— strangely cut. Indeed, they are strangely cut, in order to fit the rider properly in riding position.

wicking material next to your body as your foundation, then insulators, then something to break the wind. This is the formula for keeping warm. The wicker and wind-breaker can be single layers. Then sandwich insulators between them to construct the warm/cold barrier.

Polypropylene is valuable because it's an excellent wicker *and* insulator. It also insulates when wet. I wore polypropylene underwear during a spring rafting trip when the air temperature was in the forties and the water temperature was in the upper fifties. Even after a dunking, I stayed relatively warm. I use "polypro" for my primary insulating and wicking layer for winter cycling. Polypro also dries quickly and compresses well, so it's ideal for trips. Its cost is well within reason.

There are gloves designed for cold-weather cycling. They're well insulated and permit you to shift gears comfortably and brake with control. You can use ski gloves, too. I have no problem either braking or shifting with them, especially with today's index ("click") shifting, which just pops into place. You may even be able to use mittens. Glove liners are convenient when it gets too warm and you want to shed some of that insulation.

Don't forget about your head and ears when preparing for cold-weather cycling. I don't use anything exotic, just an earband (literally, a stretchy band that fits around your head and covers just your ears), a knit hat, or a balaclava (a head and neck covering with openings for your eyes and nose). I use the earband at temperatures from about 45 to 55 degrees, the knit hat from about 30 to 45 degrees, and the balaclava when I venture out at temperatures below 30 degrees. That's where I'm comfortable—use what works best for you, and be sure it fits comfortably inside your helmet (whose adjustable straps should accommodate it).

Very little cold-weather gear is made specifically for cycling. If you go into your local ski shop, you'll find plenty that will keep you warm, and probably at a lower temperature than what you're willing to brave on a bicycle. But you're not always upright on the bike. On a road bike, you're always bent over to some degree, even when your hands are on the top of the handlebars. So try the equipment while simulating the riding position.

Tights (also called wind tights) are great for temperatures below about 65 degrees. Muscles are more efficient and elastic when warm. Lycra tights are very comfortable, and you can even buy them with a padded crotch, so they're more like long cycling shorts. Unpadded tights are available, too, and they're wonderful for just about any activity.

Sock liners, thermal socks, and shoe covers round out the cold-weather attire. If you dress properly around your mid-section, you probably won't need to worry about keeping your feet warm until it gets below 40 degrees or so.

COMPUTER

The bicycle world's only real intersection with the electronics industry is the bike computer. It's nothing more than a digital display of (in some way or another) speed, time, and distance. Some units display cadence, heart rate, and even altitude. Computers can serve as a training aid, or just add the fun of knowing how far you've gone or how fast you're going. They have one drawback—you can get caught up watching them. I get around this by putting mine on the maximum-speed mode; the only time this changes is when you're going too fast to want to be watching the computer anyway.

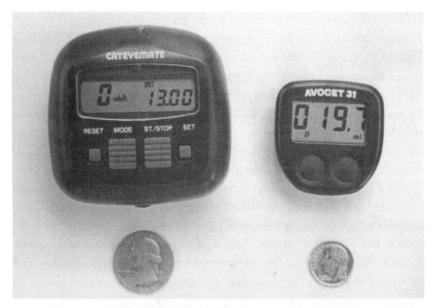

The computer at left is about eight years old. It's substantially larger than the newer, compact model shown with it, but it does offer two displays simultaneously. Both computers display speed, maximum speed, trip distance, total distance, and elapsed time. Like most computers today, the smaller one also has a clock built in.

All computers today are built to mount unobtrusively on the handlebar.

Some brands are more reliable than others, especially in wet weather. Since weather is weather, always unpredictable, it's worth asking your bike shop which computers hold up best.

PEPPER SPRAYS

These are great for warding off aggressive dogs. They work like Mace, but faster, and with far less dramatic effects. Even if you hit a dog square in the eyes, the pooch will suffer no damage at all. It will just run to the grass and wipe its eyes. Mostly, though, dogs just get a whiff of the stuff and retreat. Pepper sprays protect both the dog and the rider from traffic. Halt! is the most popular brand, and it works. It readily clips to your brake or shift cable for easy access.

TRAILERS

You can hook a trailer to the back of your bike to carry children, groceries, touring gear, etc. They're versatile and put an emphasis on safety. These trailers are becoming more popular, so your bike shop should have them.

Pepper sprays, which are effective for safely warding off aggressive dogs, can be stored in a number of convenient, easily reachable places. This one hangs in its pouch under the saddle.

The Dog's Scare. - The Cyclist's Delight.

„You press the ball, the ammonia does the rest!"

W. WASHINGTON TAYLOR & Co.,
ROTTERDAM.

Hoofdagenten der FALCON en MANHATTAN Rijwielen.

Excitable dogs have always been a minor road hazard for cyclists. Among the most bizarre accessories of the late 19th century was this dog-repellent squeeze bottle, filled with ammonia and mounted on the handlebar. Another 19th-century squeeze device for this purpose employed gunpowder to make a loud bang. And there was even a handlebar pistol for protection against highwaymen!

ACCESSORIES TO AVOID

There are some items that I consider worthless junk or downright dangerous. I'll describe them—not as a recommendation but as a warning.

Safety levers. I'd call these danger levers, but they're often called brake-extension levers because they permit braking from the top of the handlebars on road bikes. The problem is that they don't allow you full braking force. Also, your hands are toward the center of the handlebars, allowing you less steering control. If your bike is equipped with them, I advise you to remove them, buy a pair of brake-hood covers and get used to applying the brakes from on top of the brake hoods.

Radios, tape players. It should be obvious why I don't like to see riders using these items. Did you ever notice how you seldom see riders wearing helmets when they're wearing Walkmans? Does that tell you anything? Keep your senses tuned to the road. With these gadgets, you can't

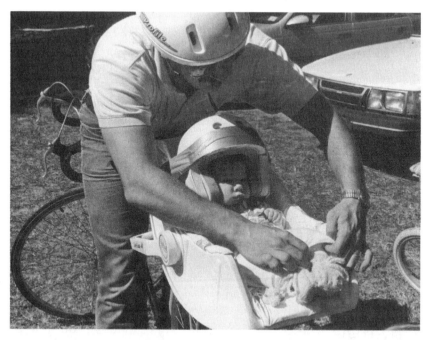

Ingenuity, with an emphasis on safety, can transform a child seat into a practical bicycle "rumble-seat." Gordon Broz (who has a patent pending for this invention) straps in his daughter Carolyn for a ride in Virginia.

No modern horns or bells will be shown in this book, because the authors (and most experts) regard sound signals useless if not downright dangerous on bicycles. By the late 1870s and early 1880s, road traffic (pedestrian, equestrian, and cycling) inspired an assortment of bicycle bells and horns such as these in an old advertisement. They've been with us ever since, though they seldom prevent collisions.

possibly give your undivided attention to traffic or tree stumps. Save your music for your stationary exercise bike and enjoy the sounds of the outdoors. Even a car horn can sound pleasant if it prevents you from getting hit.

Bells and horns. It's hard to open a catalog or read a magazine article on casual cycling that doesn't remind you that some sort of audible warning device on bikes is required by law in many areas. I don't know where these areas are, and I've never seen this law enforced. I suspect that any such laws were written no later than the early part of this century, when motor traffic was practically nonexistent and many pedestrians were simply annoyed by bikes. I'd prefer to see a rider with his hands near or on the brake levers rather than on a bell or horn, though I wouldn't want to advocate your breaking the law. Finally, streamers and spoke things that make noise are useless junk.

4

The Smart Rider

Everyone knows how to ride a bike, but some people ride much better than others. A smart rider develops rhythm which can be maintained—and quickly regained when necessary. A smart rider also respects but isn't intimidated by traffic, and knows his limitations.

BUILDING CONFIDENCE

An experienced rider casually slings a leg over his bike, slips his feet into the toe clips, and gracefully picks and meanders through brush or coexists with traffic, all with quiet, unpretentious confidence.

I've been watching a friend start cycling as an adult. Janice hasn't been on a bike in years, drives a Saab at 55 miles per hour, and always unplugs the toaster to remove the stuck toast. Garage sales and antiques excite her, and she admits to being "something of a wimp."

When my brother Peter went to Finland for a year as an exchange student, Janice borrowed his bike. Although the bike fit her well, the proper seat height made her apprehensive. Nervous, actually. She felt more confident after she lowered the seat. When she sat on the bike, the big bend in her knees looked terribly uncomfortable and inefficient to me, but to her it brought confidence.

And who was I to argue? Why spoil fun on a technicality? Three weeks later, after her confidence and trust were built, we raised the seat to its proper height (measured as described in Chapter 2), and that is where it's been ever since. Confidence is an essential learning tool.

Aesop said familiarity breeds contempt; Mark Twain said it breeds

The contentment of an easy ride has always been an attraction of cycling. This advertisement was painted by Edward Penfield in 1896.

children. But familiarity also breeds confidence. You must feel confident while riding the bike before you can feel safe on the road, and especially in traffic or on an unpredictable trail. Riding the bike for as little as five minutes begins building confidence because you've learned something you didn't know before. Once confidence is established, you're ready for versatility.

Confidence isn't free, yet you can't buy it. (Insurance isn't confidence.) The right to confidence must be earned. Although Leo Derocher or Yogi Berra never said "if ya ain't got da confidence ya ain't gonna enjoy da ride," they would have said it if they were cyclists, and they would have been right.

Confidence comes from trust, predictability, and consistency. It can't exist when you don't know or don't like what will happen next. When you know what will happen next, you'll trust the bike, and only then will you be relaxed. Then you're ready to move on to bigger things, whether they be rougher trails, higher speeds, busier roads, greater distances, or some combination thereof.

No amount of reading will replace time on the bike. Reading can prepare you for what you're about to feel and encounter, and it may excite

Confidence doesn't have to mean aggressiveness (and shouldn't outside of competitive racing). Pauline rides for relaxation and fun, which is promoted by learning how your bike will react to each situation it encounters.

and get you ready to go, but it can't replace the actual riding. Again it's like driving—know the laws and safety procedures—but you can't learn to drive in the classroom.

Even if you've done some casual bicycling, I think you'll find the following practice procedures very helpful. Find a quiet place where you can practice riding. The fewer cars, pedestrians, noises, and distractions, the better. Do what you must to be comfortable on the bike, whether it's lowering the seat as my friend did or riding only in straight lines until you know what the bike feels like. Ride slowly, never out of control. You'll find that riding up a slight grade will give you fuller control of the bike's speed.

Be honest with yourself about your abilities, and you'll become comfortable in no time. Exaggerating your abilities is lying to yourself. Be conscious of what you're doing, but don't exaggerate your limitations, either. Millions of people all over the world ride bikes every day without tension or anxiety; if they can, so can you.

BRAKING TECHNIQUES

Making the bike stop is more important than making it go. Effective braking requires even pressure on both brakes, and it's a good idea to develop this habit from the start. Many riders don't use their front brake because they fear locking the front wheel and flipping the bike. However, your front brake provides the real stopping power; your back brake keeps you from locking the front wheel by stopping the transfer of momentum. The harder you apply the front brake, the harder you must apply the rear. The rules change when you're riding on a steep trail; then there are instances where you apply only your back brake. We'll examine those instances in Chapter 8.

Just a few decades ago, bicycles routinely employed a coaster brake, or foot brake, located in the rear hub. The rider activated this brake by pedaling backward about a quarter-turn, which was as far as the crank would go. This backward rotation of the mechanism inside the rear hub activated the brake.

Today's hand brakes are incomparably safer for two reasons. First, you get more stopping power because you're able to slow your front wheel, which, as I said earlier, provides the real stopping power. Second, human hands are more accurate than human feet, and are able to control the brake pressure better, overcoming the tendency to skid.

Look at the cables leading from your two brake levers to the caliper arms (the arms on which the brake pads are mounted). Assuming they're installed in the standard manner, the lever on the left side of the handlebar operates the front wheel's brake, and the lever on the right operates the rear wheel's brake. Practice riding slowly and gently (at first) squeezing the left and right levers at the same time. The brakes may be more sensitive or have a greater mechanical advantage than you realize, so if you're unaccustomed to doing this, practice in a wide-open area clear of obstacles.

Of course, sudden emergency stops can require a bit more finesse. When braking hard, sliding your weight behind the seat will further help to prevent you from flipping over. Practice and awareness prepare you for using this emergency technique.

UNDERSTANDING GEARS

You can figure out how many gears your bike has by multiplying the number of chainrings (front sprockets) by the number of back sprockets, as explained in Chapter 1. Most mountain bikes (and even those department-store bikes that resemble mountain bikes) have three chainrings and six or seven rear sprockets, so they have 18 or 21 gear combinations, or "speeds." Racing bikes usually have 14 or 16 gear combinations, and casual bikes have 12 or more.

You shift from one gear to another by pedaling while moving a gearshift lever (there are two—one for the front sprocket set and one for the back set). The levers may be in one of four places. On road bikes, they're usually on the down tube; that's the tube that slopes at a 45-degree angle toward the pedals. On older road bikes, they can be on the handlebar stem or on the top tube, the tube you straddle when you're standing over the bike. Mountain bikes usually have the shift levers near the rider's thumb when his hands are on the grips. Often there are two levers on each side, one on top of the other, and you just "flick" these with your thumb. Flick the top lever to shift up (making the pedaling harder, but going farther with each pedal stroke), or the bottom lever to downshift (making it easier to pedal). Some mountain bikes have a ring next to each

The author controls a sudden stop by sliding rearward off the seat as he brakes. This maneuver also greatly reduces the chance of pitching over as you slow down suddenly.

hand grip, and you rotate the rings to change gears. Mountain bikes now have indicators to tell you what sprocket the chain is on.

Choosing the "right" gear mystifies many riders. It's easy to understand that shifting gears makes it easier or harder to pedal and that you choose a lower gear to climb a hill. The confusion lies in knowing which gear to choose, and why. But you can take comfort in knowing that you shift when the pedaling gets too easy or too hard.

You can't get something for nothing. Never could. If you make the bike easier to pedal, you won't travel as far with each revolution of the pedals. That's why you can pedal like crazy (in a very low gear) and seemingly go nowhere.

Pedaling isn't exempt from a natural rhythm that we succumb to when doing something repetitious. But hills and winds provide a greater (or lesser) resistance, so to maintain the rhythm, we shift gears when the resistance changes.

Let your legs tell you which gear is right. Pedal at the cadence that feels natural to you. It won't be a single cadence but a range, and you'll know that when you go up a hill you'll have to downshift because it's too hard to

You can figure out the number of gears a bicycle has by multiplying the number of front sprockets by the number of back sprockets. This one has three front sprockets and seven back sprockets, so it's a "21-speed" bike.

To shift this mountain bike, you simply push one of the levers (atop the handlebar) clockwise or counterclockwise while pedaling. The rider, Catie Elman, can easily reach the shift levers without removing her hands from the handlebar, a definite advantage on a rough trail.

pedal. When you pedal with a wind behind you, choose a higher gear, or one that takes you farther with each pedal stroke.

Many riders try to push too high a gear at too slow a cadence; I was one of them. Compare pedaling to moving a wheelbarrow full of bricks—you can move a few bricks at a time all day long, day after day, but moving the fully loaded wheelbarrow any distance soon tires you. When you're tired, you're also more susceptible to injuries. If you're riding just a short period of time, you can probably push the high gear with no ill effects. Over longer distances, you're better off shirking the macho image and taking the easy way, which many agree is somewhere between 60 and 120 pedal rpms. Most riders will be most efficient between 80 and 90 rpms.

A single-speed bike's drivetrain consists of two sprockets joined by a continuous chain. Pedals turn the front sprocket; the rear sprocket turns the back wheel. Imagine that the sprockets both have twenty teeth. When the front sprocket makes one revolution, the back must also make one revolution. And since the back sprocket is connected to the center of a wheel, the wheel also makes one revolution.

Now imagine two sprockets in the back, the second with only ten teeth, and attached to the center of the first sprocket. We can move the chain to either back sprocket, while it's always attached to the front sprocket. If we put the chain on the smaller sprocket and turn the pedals one revolution now, the back sprocket will turn twice. If the back sprocket turns twice, the back wheel turns twice, and you'll go twice as far with one turn of the pedals.

So why not put a gigantic sprocket in front and a tiny sprocket in the rear? Because you still can't get something for nothing. More energy is the expense for traveling farther with a pedal stroke.

PEDALING

Concentrate on making your feet go in circles, following the path of the pedals. "Pedaling circles" is easier to achieve when you're pedaling at a higher cadence. Toe clips help greatly by holding your foot to the pedal and letting you pull up on the pedals as well as push down. Also, the toe clips save you all the energy you'd spend keeping your feet on the pedals. Riding any distance efficiently requires toe clips (or the newer clipless pedal system), but millions of miles have been ridden without them.

Leave the toe strap loose at first. Before starting, slip one foot into its clip. Now begin riding. When you're riding steadily, flip the other pedal over with your toe so you can slip your foot into the second toe clip. This will take a little practice, but in no time you'll be able to flip that pedal and slip into the clip without thinking. The newer clipless pedal system eliminates the clip and strap.

After riding for a while, you fall into a natural rhythm. You won't notice the rhythm until you begin riding again after a break. Until you regain the rhythm, pedaling will feel a bit awkward; you may even think something is wrong with the bike, or that you're tired. The smart rider, aware of what's happening, will continue to ride, concentrating on smooth pedaling, perhaps even gearing down to help regain the rhythm. You'll regain your rhythm within a few minutes without realizing it, and will then maintain it until you stop and start again.

5

Coping with Traffic and Road Hazards

Many of the rules and techniques for cycling in traffic are a matter of common sense, but not all of them are obvious. The more you ride, the more adept you'll become, but I've seen experienced riders do foolish things. I trust you won't ride in traffic until you're confident about maintaining control of the bike, especially while stopping and avoiding obstacles. As with driving a car, it can't all be learned by reading a book. However, I can share with you the important rules I've obeyed for years.

You can't eliminate all traffic from your cycling route, and it can be awfully scary trying to turn left on a four-lane highway with large steel vehicles traveling at fifty miles per hour. It's important to develop a healthy respect for cars. Don't be intimidated by them, just respect them. Riding a mountain bike in the woods may be the only way to escape traffic, but even when you're riding on a bike trail, you may encounter pedestrian traffic, so you must learn to cope with obstacles.

Cars and bikes use roads in different ways. Cars head for the highways with dashed lines and guardrails, and connect them with slower, smaller crossroads. Bikes must sometimes travel from one country lane or road to another by using a busy highway. Encounters with traffic are inevitable, so let's explore ways to make these necessary evils manageable.

RULE #1:
YOU CAN'T RIDE EVERYWHERE

Stay off the interstates and similar divided highways. Cars don't expect to see bikes there, traffic moves very fast, and often these highways are illegal for anything other than motorized vehicles. This isn't a bad thing; such roads simply aren't designed for bikes.

Avoiding these roads may be obvious, yet I'm often asked if I ride on them. I don't, of course. I keep to the secondary roads, which will take you just about anywhere you want to go. Look at your road map, and you'll easily find alternative routes. Usable service roads often parallel and are more scenic than big highways. The air is easier to breathe, too.

RULE #2:
RIDE WITH TRAFFIC

Always, always cycle with traffic, never against it, and always ride in single file. For purposes of traffic regulation, a bicycle is considered a motor vehicle in most states, and the law says bicycles must ride on the right side of the road, which is where motorists expect to see them. Generally speaking, stay as far to the right as possible. Roads with a smooth, wide shoulder are a blessing, even when heavily traveled.

Sometimes "as far to the right as possible" means on the white line. Shoulders aren't always present, and even when they're wide, they're often broken or have much loose gravel. Mountain bikes have a definite advantage over road bikes here; the ATB's thicker tires handle these obstacles far better than the thin tires on the road bike.

Riding as far to the right as possible will give you the safest and most courteous place on the road, provided there is no cross traffic (see Rule #5). You won't hold up traffic, even if a motorist doesn't see you until the last minute.

In the city, where cars are parked along the side of the road, the bicycle's informal lane is one to two feet away from the parked cars. J-walking pedestrians, side-view mirrors, limited maneuvering space (for both bike and car), opening car doors, and cars exiting from their parking spaces are some of the hazards you may encounter when riding in the city.

Because of these hazards, you can't look behind you as often as you may want to. Mirrors help greatly, and so does listening. If you're approaching a pothole, just knowing whether or not something is behind you tells you whether it's safe to maneuver around it or if you must face it head on.

RULE #3:
BE PREDICTABLE

You never want to surprise a car. Or a pedestrian, or a truck, or a dog. (Well, sometimes a dog.) I can't stress enough the importance of being predictable.

In order to be predictable you must be seen. Locking eyes with a driver isn't always enough. Sometimes a bike just doesn't register as being "important" to motorists, and they unconsciously ignore it. You must safeguard against these intrusions of your right of way by simply being aware of what may happen and having an escape plan. It doesn't matter whose fault it is if you get hit; you won't win.

A motorist slows down because he's not sure of what you intend to do. This may seem like a blessing, but the uncertainty makes him wary, takes more of your concentration, slows down everyone behind him, and thus causes a build-up of traffic, all of which you're trying to avoid. Your goal is to ride in a predictable manner, far to the right, obeying traffic laws, signaling when you must. Take the right-of-way when it's yours, and when you're sure it's safe. Don't let confidence on the bike lead to overconfidence in traffic.

RULE #4:
USE HAND SIGNALS THAT WORK

Using your hands and arms to indicate the direction that you intend to go is a good way to eliminate any question any driver or pedestrian has in regard to the direction that you want to go. I use five signals—one for left, right, straight ahead, stop, and to wave traffic around me.

Signal before you begin to slow down. Don't try to signal while you're braking—it's too easy to lose control. When a car is behind you at a red traffic light, signal before you pull out, even if it's obvious why you're in the middle of the lane. The driver may wonder why you're out there. Also, make the signals as clear as possible.

To indicate left or right, I simply stick out the appropriate arm and point in the direction I want to go.

Using your left arm for the right turn signal was necessary for motorists

The purpose of any signal is to communicate the rider's intention, instantly and clearly. This photo illustrates proper signaling. It will be clear to any motorist, pedestrian, or another cyclist what she intends to do.

fifty years ago, before left and right signal lights on cars were standard. The driver would have needed a right arm eight feet long to stick it through the passenger's side window. The driver therefore stuck out his left arm, bent it straight up at the elbow, and sometimes pointed right with his hand. Long ago I abandoned using this signal—it's too awkward and not clear enough. In the bent-over riding position, your left arm angles forward and no one can see it. To signal a right turn, simply stick out your right arm and point.

To indicate straight ahead, I point one arm straight out in front of me, at about a 45-degree upward angle. This is beneficial when you're in the right-hand lane and you want to indicate you're not turning right. I use my right arm because I feel more confident braking with just my left hand if necessary. Keep in mind, though, that your left hand controls the front brake, and without using the back brake, you can more easily lock up the front wheel and pitch the bike over.

My stop signal is rarely to tell motorists that I'm stopping, but rather to tell them not to pass me, such as on a windy road with narrow curves, or anywhere that I have a better view of the oncoming traffic and road situations than the car behind me. This I indicate by sticking my left arm out and down at a 45-degree angle, fingers spread.

I also wave traffic around me when I'm sure it's safe for cars to pass. If it's not safe for traffic to pass, and a car does so anyway, the cyclist is in just as much danger as the motorist.

RULE #5:
ACT LIKE A CAR AT
INTERSECTIONS—USUALLY

Trouble most often occurs at intersections. Let's say cars traveling in the same direction as you are waiting to turn left, yielding to oncoming traffic. While a driver is holding up traffic, others behind him get impatient and try to pass him on the right, which is your lane. Oncoming traffic is turning left in front of you. Even traffic that's moving in the same direction as you are can be turning right, again crossing your lane.

The shoulder (if there is one) is your lane, but you have no way of claiming and protecting it with any commanding authority. Traffic is always crossing your lane, to which they have the right. Trouble starts when motorists don't see you; you're often eclipsed by other cars. Or perhaps an oncoming car is gauging the speed and distance of the car he must turn in front of or behind. These obstacles all contribute to the motorists ignoring you for more important things that can dent his car.

Look at the accompanying illustration, in which the car lanes are divided into four bike lanes. The far right 4 lane extends from the white line to the grassy edge of a shoulder. The far left 1 lane will require more explanation.

The 4 lane is the safest and most often used bike lane. Cars expect to see you there. Use this lane when there are no intersections, and for any right turn. Use your hand signals to clarify your intentions.

The 3 lane is also a "going straight" lane, but used at an intersection. When you're in this lane, and using your hand signals, you clearly indicate that you're going straight and have no intention of turning right. The 3 position is particularly valuable to make sure a car on a crossroad sees you and is aware of your intentions—but I still use hand signals at

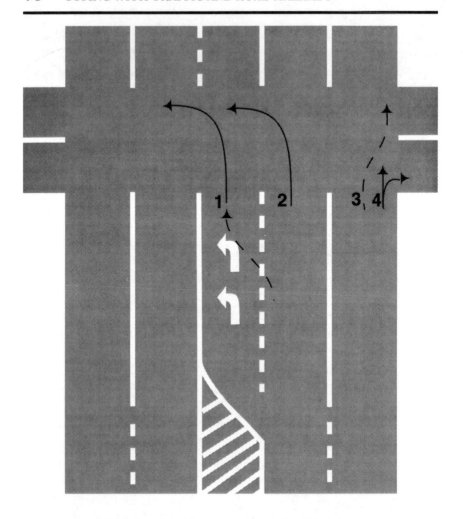

intersections to remove any hint of doubt in the driver's mind as to exactly what my intentions are.

Often you can't get to the 3 lane because of heavy traffic, so you're stuck in 4. Traffic that's traveling with you and turning right can easily cut you off, so you must make sure you aren't caught beside a car while going through an intersection. Adjust your speed so you're riding through the intersection when you're parallel with the space *between* the two cars passing you, not next to one, and signal that you're going straight ahead.

You can also turn left from the 3 lane, but only on a road where two lanes are going in the same direction and left turns are permitted (see illustration on page 62).

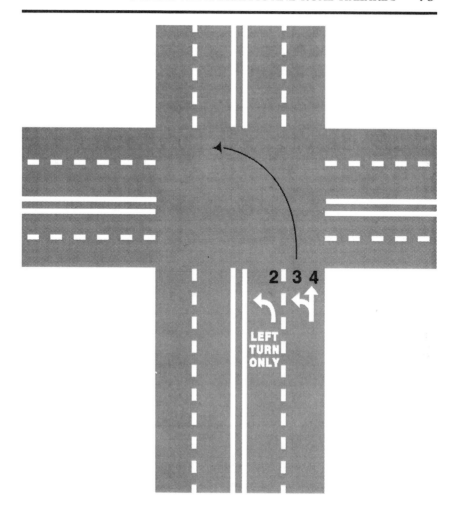

Here, the left lane is always the left turn lane (although cars may go straight). Turn left by starting from the 3 lane of the car's passing lane and heading toward the corner where the two roads meet. You want to wind up in the 4 lane of the road onto which you're turning. Don't be surprised if cars that are turning left pass you in the intersection. You're in the 3 lane so they can pass you. By going directly to the 4 lane you shouldn't be in their way.

The 2 lane is your "turning left" lane when cycling on a two-lane road. Your path here is to start in the 2 lane and wind up in the 4 lane of the four-lane road onto which you're turning. Aim for the corner where the two roads join. The same right-of-way rules apply here as they do for a car.

If you must wait to make this turn because you're yielding to oncoming traffic, stay in the 3 lane and pull straight ahead into the middle of the intersection. Don't pull so far forward that you'll obstruct oncoming traffic from making a left turn. When it's safe for you to turn, proceed to the 4 lane of the road onto which you're turning.

The 1 lane covers the leftmost part of the road. It is seldom used, but is akin to riding on the white line in the 4 lane. Use this lane when the road you're on "grows" a "left-turn-only" lane near the traffic signal. These are often heavily traveled roads where traffic can easily back up a hundred yards from a red light. You seldom have the luxury of going from the 4 lane directly to the left-turn-only lane, so you need a safe place to ride until you reach the left-turn-only lane. Once in the left-turn-only lane, follow the rule for turning left from the 2 or 3 lane.

When you want to turn left on very busy roads, it's often easiest to do so by staying in the 4 lane until you get to the intersection; then turn right, make a U-turn a safe distance from the intersection, and simply go straight through the intersection in the 4 lane.

RULE #6:
KNOW WHAT'S AROUND YOU

This includes anything moving or capable of moving, plus the accesses for things moving. Riding along city streets where cars are parked adds obstacles. Seeing the exhaust of a parked car means the motor's running and the car may move. Someone sitting on the driver's side may open a door. If you can't see the crossroad coming up because your view is obstructed by parked cars, a driver at that intersection can't see you, either. A pedestrian may emerge from between two parked cars with a bag of groceries blocking his view.

Determining that traffic is behind you isn't quite as simple as it sounds. If you simply turned your head and looked over your left shoulder, you'd veer to the left, possibly into the path of a truck. When you turn your head that far, you tend to turn your shoulders, too, which ultimately turns your handlebars and tilts your body; this in turn leans the bike and causes it to veer.

Since you're really interested in what's immediately behind you, turn your head (no more than 45 degrees) just far enough to the left to see if any traffic is near you. When you know nothing is there, you can turn more. You still want to master riding in a straight line while glancing behind you, but now if you veer left, you won't get hit. Rear-

If you turn your head too far around to see what's behind you, your body will tend to lean sideward and you'll probably veer into traffic.

Turn only your head, and only as far sideward as necessary—never more than 90 degrees to the left—to see what's immediately behind you or alongside. Do it like this and you can continue to move forward in a straight line.

view mirrors are available, and they can be a big help when you must ride in traffic.

Experience will teach you to cock your head slightly so you can listen for what's approaching instead of hearing the wind rush past your ears, a technique especially helpful on quiet roads.

Some motorists considerately honk when they're about fifty yards behind you, alerting you that they're coming. (Some motorists will honk when they're three yards away, scaring the daylights out of you.) When you're sure a car's behind you, don't turn around; you know the car's approaching. There may be a car immediately behind you. Just wait for it to pass. Sometimes I'll stick my left hand out to show appreciation and signal the car to pass me.

Forethought is another important tool; envision what will happen next, or two steps ahead. If you're riding in a line of traffic that's approaching an intersection, look two cars ahead, but don't forget about the car directly in front of you.

RULE #7:
TAKE THE RIGHT OF WAY WHEN IT'S YOURS...

...but only when you're sure it's safe. All in-traffic riding demands some trust in drivers. Taking the right of way pushes that trust a little further. You'll take it, but only when you're sure you trust the driver. After you're sure he's seen you, anyway.

Taking the right of way is a part of being predictable, and it's more essential than many riders realize. Motorists also gain a healthier respect for what is rightfully the cyclist's. However, don't risk getting hit by *demanding* your right of way. You won't win anything.

Understand that most motorists will respect bicycles if the bikes don't create an unnecessary obstacle. Certainly you'll encounter intolerant drivers, but as I said before, it doesn't matter whose fault it is if you get hit. I often hear stories from riders who complain about the insensitive motorists who hate bicycles on the road. Since my own experience has been far more pleasant, I can only surmise that their riding practices hold up, frustrate, and annoy motorists.

Consider the motorists' point of view. Most will tolerate bicycles if the bikes are doing what they can to avoid being a nuisance. I've seen cyclists riding two abreast in traffic, not using the shoulder, without regard for who's behind them; these are the same riders who complain about inconsiderate motorists. If you're one of these riders, please stop; you're making the rest of us take the blame. Cars have a right to the road, too.

I've ridden into Washington, D.C., on a Friday at three o'clock in the afternoon and had no trouble at all. The road was four lanes wide with constant traffic and no shoulder. And there was road construction. By staying far to the right and being respectful of the steel vehicles being driven at fifty miles per hour by people who wanted to get home, I cycled unharrassed, even though my bike was effectively widened by the panniers (touring bags) that carried my gear.

ROUGH SURFACES AND ROAD HAZARDS

Road hazards include puddles, cinders, steel-grate bridges, and many other obstacles that add to already confining traffic situations. Even without traffic, these hazards can cause you to fall. I'll list some of the more common hazards I've encountered, and how I handle them.

Open-grate steel bridges. These are very slippery when wet. I know—I fell on one. After I fell, as I was sliding across the bridge, my little finger got stuck in one of the grates, and I was injured. Ride these bridges slowly. In wet weather, walk your bike across.

Potholes. The hazard is apparent. It can mess up you and your bike. Ride around the hole if this won't interfere with traffic. If you must cross a pothole, do it slowly.

Puddles. An innocent-looking puddle may be a pothole filled with water. If you must ride through a puddle because of traffic, do so with great caution and expect a jolt.

Loose gravel or cinders. Your bike can easily slide out from under you, especially when going around corners. Gravel and cinders are especially present during snowy winters and early spring. Slow down *before* you hit gravel or cinders, because braking on loose materials can be hazardous.

Shiny patches on the road. In the summer they're probably just tar. In the winter they could be ice. Don't ride on ice. Walk your bike.

Wooden bridges. When they're wet, these can be as slippery as steel-grate bridges. The same procedures apply.

Sewer grates. Some are positioned so the bars that form the grate are parallel with the road. This is a perfect coin/slot relationship, in which the wheel is the coin. Don't ride over them.

Wooden bridges may be scenic, but they're very slippery when wet, as are bridges with steel-grate surfaces, common in many parts of the country. Ride slowly and with caution on either type of bridge and, if it's slippery, dismount and walk your bike over.

There are many other hazards; you must pay attention any time you're riding your bike.

One note should be added concerning tractor-trailers. Truck drivers are often presented with very difficult situations, so consider their position. During a West Virginia tour, I had just reached the bottom of a mountain pass when I heard a truck far behind me blowing his air horn. The white lines on the road were up against the guard rail on one side and a mountainside on the other. As the driver got closer, his horn sounded more emphatic. I continued to ride as close to the guard rail as I could, but my bike was made wider by my panniers. The air horn stopped only when the truck was just behind me, and he finally zoomed by, displacing tidal waves of air that pushed me around the way a rough sea tosses a swimmer. I was annoyed that he sped by so fast, and that his air horn didn't quit. But when he was well beyond me, I smelled the

Because mountain bikes are rugged and stable, they're particularly well suited to jumping curbs or riding off them. This boy may be practicing tricks, but more likely he's just undaunted by the curb and in no danger of losing his balance.

strong, unmistakable odor of burnt brake linings. That driver probably had very little braking power, and on such a narrow road! He had every right to tell me to get out of the way, and I still commend him for keeping that big truck under control. I could have been flattened.

My best move would have been to stop the bike and pull it over the guard rail. I learned from this experience, but it shows that you must consider everything in traffic. The bicycle and motor vehicle can co-exist on the roads. Each has its place. But no one wins a showdown.

CAN TRICK RIDING
BE CONDONED?

I'll bet there hasn't been a boy with a bike who hasn't tried to impress a girl with trick riding. Cyclists—especially young ones—like to jump curbs, "pop wheelies," ride backward, and ride in the "look-Ma-no-hands" style. They always have and they always will.

But a couple of points must be made. Every one of these tricks is idiotic where there's any traffic at all—they can and do cause fatalities.

Where there's no traffic whatever (maybe in a vacant parking lot, for example) such tricks can be harmless fun. You simply must be aware of the risks. While it can be argued that these tricks can improve your balance, more than a few riders have followed the "look-Ma-no-hands" trick by scraping themselves off the ground and crying, "Look, Ma, no teeth!" Always wear your helmet.

6

Training

You've been riding around your neighborhood for some time now, and you're itching for longer, more interesting rides. But your muscles and backside argue. You want the goal to be more ambitious, but realize your physical assets need modernizing. Getting new muscles and rump isn't feasible, so you decide to upgrade the present resources through training.

WHAT IS BEING "IN SHAPE"?

Being in shape, being fit, being conditioned—they all mean the same thing—isn't difficult for a healthy person. It feels wonderful. You're livelier because you have more energy. You're happier, and your overall state of mind improves. Of course you're healthier. You're more confident, and little things don't bother you.

Being in shape isn't necessarily dependent on your weight, or how slender or muscular you are. Those Russian Olympic powerlifters who ate four whole chickens for breakfast certainly weren't pictures of health, but only a track star would dare to criticize them. An amateur athlete may be able to cycle ten miles in forty-five minutes but wants to decrease his time to a half-hour, so is he in shape or not? The answer depends on your goal, which doesn't have to be specific. If you've been inactive for many years, your only goal may be to feel better, lose weight, or invest in your health's future. Fine. That's a banner first step. The second step requires action, but after a word of medical advice.

It's always a good idea to see your doctor before starting an exercise program. According to the Mayo Clinic *Family Health Book*, it's essential "if you are obese, lead a largely sedentary life, or are over age 40; if you have diabetes, a kidney disorder, or other serious health problem or had a relative who died of a heart attack before age fifty; or if you smoke or suffer from high blood pressure." Your doctor may prescribe a stress test, or just suggest what activities will benefit you most.

THE RIGHT MINDSET

Getting in shape is easy; staying in shape is harder. Whereas getting in shape requires only enthusiasm, staying in shape demands discipline—piano lessons and diets aren't the only New Year's resolutions given up by Lent. We're like kids who lose interest in a new toy—that's why it's essential to find an activity that you'll enjoy as a lifelong pursuit.

Simply riding your bike or walking briskly is enjoyable, and obviously more beneficial than sitting in your armchair. The discipline kicks you out of your armchair when you feel like snoozing instead. I need that kick

Your health and fitness can be improved at any age. This couple could just as easily have driven their car to the beach, but cycling feels good, and riding is, in itself, one of the best exercises for maintaining fitness.

sometimes, even though I know it takes about five pedal strokes for me to smile and wonder why I didn't start earlier. It feels that good. In fact, I think I'll go for a ride now; I can write when it's dark out. Go ahead—take your bike out. You can read when it gets dark. That's the mindset that will get and keep you in good enough condition for hours of cycling without undue effort or fatigue.

GETTING USED TO THE SEAT

The biggest complaint I hear, and one I experience myself, is rump discomfort, the problem of being able to stay on the seat for as long as you (or I) want to ride. My butt hurts long before my legs and lungs say they've had enough. During a pleasant February weekend I tried to ride two days in a row, but on the second day I had to pad the saddle with my wool hat because my butt was so sore. Compare cycling again to driving your car—you may have enough money to drive across the country, but if sitting in your car for more than an hour gives you a backache, you have a problem to solve before leaving your driveway.

So, at the beginning of your riding season, cycle once a week for about an hour. Make sure your seat is properly adjusted (see Chapters 1 and 2), and forget about speed or distance. Pedal easily, but constantly—when you stop pedaling, you tend to support your weight with your legs, and lift slightly off the seat. You can't get used to the seat if you're not sitting on it. Also, your aerobic capacity won't increase if you're just coasting.

After the first three weeks, ride two or three times per week for as long as you want, or can. Don't worry about riding for too long—at worst you'll have a sore backside. After a few weeks, you may be surprised at how you barely notice the seat anymore. You won't be able to ride across the country yet—you're still building your mileage base. But your seat time will naturally increase as you continue to ride. If you still get sore, try lowering your seat about an inch; then, as you get used to it, gradually raise it over the next few weeks to the proper height.

Or get a better seat—the gel seats are excellent. Many are available in both men's and women's styles, and there are gel touring, racing, and mountain-bike seats. Touring seats are designed for the rider who spends long hours in the saddle, day after day. I use a gel touring seat on my racing bike as well as my touring bike, because it's just right for me.

Cycling shorts also help. They're more than just fad shorts that fashion dictates. Bona fide cycling shorts have a pad in the crotch, and they're cut to fit correctly in the riding position (see Chapter 3).

NUTRITION

Both athlete and spectator benefit from a balanced diet. But exercising uses more calories than a sedentary lifestyle, so the extra calories must be replaced (unless your goal is to lose weight). I'd love to be able to tell you there's a miracle diet that will enable you to perform at your peak all the time, but it doesn't exist. To complicate matters, what works best for me may not be anything special for you, and the system that works for me today may only sometimes work tomorrow! Luckily, there are some guidelines that nearly everyone agrees on.

Carbohydrates are the fuel most efficiently used by your muscles. According to the University of California at Berkeley *Wellness Encyclopedia,* 55 to 60 percent of your calories should come from carbohydrates, and endurance athletes should increase that to 60 to 70 percent. Complex carbohydrates, such as grains and starches, should provide most of these calories, and no more than 15 percent should come from sugars.

Protein builds and takes care of your tissues. Your body uses it for energy when carbohydrates and fats aren't available. Regardless of your athletic intensity, about 12 to 15 percent of your calories should come from proteins. Unused protein only gets stored as fat.

Everything we don't burn gets stored as fat, so this is our most plentiful fuel. This is also the fuel we rely on when exercising for a long period of time. But a high-fat diet isn't good—no more than one-third of your calories should come from fat. If you remember that one gram of fat contains nine calories, you can easily figure out how many calories of a given food comes from fat: Multiply the fat grams by nine, divide this product by the total number of calories, and multiply by 100. The result is the percentage of calories that come from fat. So, if a 200-calorie serving contains 5 grams of fat, fat contributes 22.5 percent of those 200 calories.

One of the biggest differences between the good athlete and the super athlete is the percentage of body fat. Lower body fat enables the body to tolerate heat better, provides a greater power-to-weight ratio, and can improve your cardiovascular performance. Fat hinders you because it insulates the body, acts as dead weight, and causes the body to process

Learn to drink while you're riding. You must replace the fluids lost through perspiration, even on cool days, to avoid dehydration.

oxygen less efficiently. These factors cause you to waste energy that could be going toward powering your bike.

Vitamins and minerals help your body use fuels—the carbohydrates, proteins, and fats. However, if your diet is well-balanced and high in complex carbs, you probably don't need supplements.

Let's sum it all up. Food is your fuel, like gas is a car's fuel. Some cars are finicky about the gas they use, others are more resilient. Some cars are designed to run on high-octane fuel, but will still function on the regular stuff. Some owners will even tell you their cars prefer certain brands of fuel. You're the same way—if eating a special diet makes you feel better, or the numbers say you perform better, that's the diet for you. And if you can eat donuts before a century ride and do okay, fine. But I'll still encourage you to avoid fats, carry bananas while you ride, eat a few pasta suppers before a long ride, and eat something light that won't sit in your stomach before riding hard, because this is what works for me, and it works for a lot of people.

You'll probably find that what you eat is most important before riding long or hard, say a century, a multi-day tour, or a race. So enjoy that piece of cake or the glass of beer, even if you're in training, but be aware of its effects. If you're really serious about it, you'll find out what works best for you. If you just want to increase your cardiovascular fitness, you probably won't notice much difference either way.

Regardless of the type of exercise you're doing, you're going to sweat, and you must replace what you lose. Mostly it's water, although you lose some electrolytes also. It's vitally important to replace this fluid, as dehydration is a dangerous thing. Plain water works fine, although such beverages as Gatorade will replace the electrolytes you lose through sweating and get into your system faster. Some even contain a bit of salt to encourage you to drink periodically while working. That's fine for most people, although those on a low-sodium diet in accordance with a doctor's advice will have to monitor their intake.

ENDURANCE

Increasing your endurance is the bread and butter of bicycling for fitness, and for all casual aerobic activities. It's essential in any weight-control program, and is most beneficial for your body. Good endurance can permit you to cycle out of the neighborhood, and the state.

Increase your endurance with aerobic exercise. Aerobic exercise doesn't necessarily entail hopping on mats to music. It's any exercise that increases your breathing rate and depth, thus benefitting your heart. Increasing the efficiency of your heart and lungs to use oxygen is a major factor in allowing you to cycle as long as you wish. And of course, cycling is, in itself, excellent aerobic exercise.

Now, how hard should you cycle? Increase your endurance by elevating your pulse to your "target rate" for at least 20 minutes. At your target heart rate, your heart beats fast enough so you derive aerobic benefit, but not fast enough to load it with undue stress. During conditioning exercises, your pulse should be 50 to 80 percent of your maximum heart rate; 70 percent is good for most people. Determine your target heart rate by first finding your maximum heart rate, as explained below, then taking 70 percent of the max rate.

Your pulse can be felt strongly at the carotid artery. The carotid pulse is located directly to each side of your Adam's apple.

Find your maximum heart rate by subtracting your age from 220. For example, a 45-year-old's maximum heart rate is 220 minus 45, or 175. Seventy percent of 175 is 123 beats per minute, so 123 bpm is your target rate. A forty-five-year-old person maintaining this pulse for at least twenty minutes will attain aerobic benefit. The longer you sustain the elevated pulse, the more aerobic benefit you'll derive. As long as you have no health problems, don't be afraid to push it. It's okay to hurt a little, and many find that the "hurt" actually feels pretty good! (But don't forget my advice about checking with your doctor before beginning your fitness program.)

Personally, I find twenty minutes of cycling more of a cruel, frustrating tease than a legitimate workout. A minimum of thirty minutes is more reasonable, and I like to have at least an hour. This gives me enough time to develop a rhythm and feel good about cycling. Remember, you're gaining aerobic benefit when your pulse is at your target rate for twenty minutes.

A lower resting pulse rate may indicate you're getting into better shape, but

Squats are an excellent exercise for strengthening the quadriceps, the large, powerful muscle at the front of the thigh—an important muscle for cycling. As Rosario Jaramillo shows here, the squat should be just so low and no lower—don't lower the buttocks below the knees.

your recovery time is a more reliable indicator. Recovery time is how long it takes your pulse to return to normal after a hard workout. When you first begin your exercise program, it may take you a full day for your resting pulse rate to return to normal, depending on what shape you're in to start with. As you get more fit, you'll recover faster. In the 1989 Tour de France, Laurent Fignon mentioned that his pulse rate was a high (for him) 60 beats per minute on the morning of the final time trial, indicating he hadn't recovered from the severe work he had done in the mountains. He proceeded to lose his 53-second lead to Greg LeMond, and thus lost the Tour.

STRENGTHENING EXERCISES

Strengthening, or anaerobic, exercises have merit, too. Strong muscles can propel you faster up hills, and with less fatigue. Lifting weights offers little benefit to your heart and lungs, but is an excellent way to increase your strength. Concentrate on your lower body to improve your climbing and sprinting, but overall weight training will be most beneficial. Squats, leg presses, toe raises, and leg curls will be beneficial.

You don't have to lift hundreds of pounds to increase your strength. Even lifting light weight with the proper technique will make you stronger and improve your muscle tone.

Use great care when using free weights. It's a good idea to have a friend around in case you get into trouble. Also, consult a book on weight lifting for proper form and safety.

Some people feel they'll automatically look like body builders if they lift weights. Not true. Body builders work specifically at building their bodies—just lifting weights won't do it. This is especially true for women. Women can get stronger and leaner, but even female body builders need steroids to develop large muscles. Women simply build muscles differently from men.

FLEXIBILITY

Twenty years ago we "limbered up"; today we "stretch out." It's all the same—increasing flexibility makes your muscles more elastic. Being flexible helps your muscles avoid the strain that athletics can place on them, and slightly elevates your pulse. It's a good way to warm up for an activity. It's important to stretch after your activity, too, as part of your cool-down.

Cycling requires a limited range of motion, so stretching provides flexibility "artificially." Flexibility is important for avoiding injuries. A fall can quickly contort your body—a flexible body will sustain fewer injuries and recover faster.

Never bounce when you stretch. The opposing muscle instinctively wants to pull the overextended limb back, so you counter the stretch. Rather, ease into the stretch, and, when you feel the pull, hold for a slow twenty-count. Relax for a few seconds, then repeat twice more.

Side stretch. Stand with feet 12 inches apart. Raise one arm above your head and slide your other arm down the outside of the leg. Don't bend forward. Repeat for the other side. Feel the stretch in your sides.

Side Stretch   **Shoulder Stretch**

Shoulder stretch. Raise arms and interlock fingers, palms up. Tuck chin and pull arms as far up and back as possible. Feel the stretch in your shoulders and sides.

Quads stretch. Use wall for support. Stand, bend right knee, and grasp ankle with right hand. Arch your back while gently pulling ankle toward buttocks. Repeat for left side. Feel the stretch in the front of your thighs.

Hamstring stretch. Sit on the floor, one leg extended in front of you, opposite heel to your buttocks. Keeping your back straight, reach toward the toes of your extended leg. Feel the stretch in the back of the thigh of your extended leg.

Calf stretch. Stand 18 inches from the wall with your feet 12 inches apart. Place palms on the wall, and, keeping your back aligned, lean

Quads Stretch

Hamstring Stretch
(alternate method)

into the wall. Feel the stretch in the back of your calf.

Inner-thigh stretch. Crouch while keeping your back straight. Put hands on knees and extend one leg to the side. Lean toward the bent knee and feel the stretch on the inside thigh of the extended leg.

Hip and back stretch. Lie on your back and bring both knees to your chest. Grab both knees with your hands and pull your face to your knees. Feel the stretch in your hips and lower back.

STAYING IN SHAPE OFF SEASON

It's easy to get out of shape through inactivity when the weather isn't conducive to riding. You can cycle in cold weather (see the section on

Calf Stretch   **Inner-thigh Stretch**

cold-weather accessories in Chapter 3), but serious riding or training when there's snow on the ground is virtually impossible. Luckily, staying in shape is easy with the right equipment or program, which can focus around cycling or other aerobic activity. You'll also tone the muscles you're working.

One word of precaution when buying exercise equipment. If you don't enjoy using the equipment, you won't use it. This applies not only to the actual activity, but to the quality of the machine. A solid, quiet, smooth-operating machine will get used. A cheaper unit may initially work acceptably, but eventually it may become creaky, unsmooth, and may not even function correctly. I bought a rower that I now hate to use because it's creaky and loses resistance once the "shock absorbers" heat up, so I seldom use it.

A rowing machine is excellent for staying in shape during the off-season. Rowers are easy to use and practical to store. This one fits into a closet corner.

The same staying-in-shape rules apply for the substitute exercises. Exercise to 70 percent of your maximum heart rate for at least 20 minutes, preferably 30, at least three times per week. The benefits you'll derive will be the same, too.

INDOOR EXERCISE EQUIPMENT

You can pick up a pot by the handle, and you can hold the pot still with the handle while you stir its contents. Your bike is comparable—you can easily use it indoors during the off-season to stay in shape and stay used to your seat by using rollers and wind trainers. Rollers simulate the road, but here the "road" moves instead of the bike. Your bike's back tire fits between two 4^{1}/$_{2}$-inch-diameter cylinders (rollers). The front tire sits on a third cylinder, which is connected to the nearest back cylinder by a belt. When you pedal your bike, its back tire turns, which turns the two back cylinders. One of these cylinders turns the belt, which drives the front cylinder, which turns your front wheel. Since both your wheels are turning, you can balance the bike as when you're riding on the road.

You just place your bike on the rollers and remove it when you're finished—no clamping is needed (although you can buy a front wheel brace that holds the bike upright so you don't have to worry about riding off the rollers when you want an easier workout). Many rollers fold for convenient storage.

You must balance and steer the bike, which is initially tricky on a 15-inch-wide "road." Stick with it. Once you get used to them, rollers are a wonderful training aid. You're positioned on the bike exactly as you'd ride on the road, so you stay used to the seat and improve your balance and technique—important factors when you actually ride. There's no wind to cheat, but you can buy a resistance unit for many rollers. And you're forced to pedal smoothly, which will benefit any rider.

Wind trainers brace your bike—there's no need to balance—and apply resistance by a fan or magnetic resistance unit to your back wheel. The resistance the fans provide is actual wind resistance, so the faster the fan spins, the more resistance there is. The magnetic units provide similar resistance—the faster they spin, the greater the generated magnetic field or eddy current, and thus the greater opposition.

Both can provide a tougher workout than unresisted rollers, but they can be more inconvenient because many wind trainers require removing the front wheel to mount the bike. Removing today's quick-release wheels—and even the screw-lock, slow-release wheels—is easy, but the less work we must do to prepare to exercise, the more apt we are to actually exercise. If you can, leave the bike on the wind trainer for the winter. You may stay used to your seat if you use the wind trainer through the winter.

Stationary bikes provide benefits similar to those you'll get when using the wind trainer, but stationary bikes usually position you much differently than your real bike will, so you probably won't stay used to

When riding rollers, you need something to grab or lean against with one arm, because you can't reach the floor with your foot. This roller is positioned so the handlebar is near a post that can be quickly grabbed.

To stay on the rollers while pedaling (without holding onto a support) you must steer, just as if you were riding on the road. It's a little tricky at first, but with practice you'll do it as easily as if you really were on the road.

the seat. Some stationary bikes get your upper body into the action by providing movable "handlebars" which help drive the resistance. This dual-action mechanism makes it easier to reach your target pulse rate because more muscles now require oxygen, so your heart must work harder.

Cross-country ski machines and rowers provide benefits similar to dual-action stationary bikes. Cross-country ski machines provide very smooth, predictable motions, and so are easy on your body. Rowers can strain your lower back, but otherwise provide an excellent workout. Steppers and treadmills also provide aerobic workout, but will tone only parts of the lower body.

OTHER ACTIVITIES

It may be too difficult to run on roads in the winter, but sometimes you can find an indoor track. For best results, use a good pair of running shoes and run on a soft surface to lessen the impact to your knees and shins—concrete is the biggest offender. Be sure to include stretching in your running routine, especially during the cool-down stage. It's better to stretch when you're already warmed up than when you're ice cold. Take it easy until you're warm.

If it's too nasty out to run, consider jumping rope. The motion for rope work is like running in place, while "running through" the rope. It's really quite a workout. See if you can do it for just five minutes.

A brisk walk is a wonderful exercise we often overlook. It's an excellent form of low-impact exercise that almost anyone can do almost anywhere. Overweight folks who wish to lose weight must incorporate an exercise program with their diet, and walking is an excellent way to start. Walking is great after a meal, before relaxing for the night—it increases your metabolism, which will help you digest your food before you sleep. Families will benefit much more from an hour's walk together than crashing in front of the television at seven o'clock.

Ice skating and roller skating are great because they use the same muscles as cycling. Eric Heiden became a well-known bike racer to complement his skating fame.

You can often play racket sports such as racquetball, tennis, squash, and paddle tennis when cycling is inaccessible. Check your area phone book for indoor courts. The only disadvantage is that you must often be a member of the racket club to play, and some of the memberships can be expensive.

Try volleyball, too. Many areas now have various levels of competitive volleyball leagues.

Advanced conditioning lets you reach fitness levels you didn't think you could attain. You have to work for it, but it can be done. Advanced conditioning requires everything that normal conditioning demands, but more, and stricter regimens. Dedication and commitment team with discipline. I choose my hardest course on days when I feel the worst.

7

Touring

Tremendous satisfaction and unusual consequences spring from taking a trip on your bicycle. "I did that!" you'll enthusiastically remember, still impressed with yourself long after the trip. Everyday obstacles, even extraordinary ones, aren't so troubling anymore. You feel mentally stronger and more independent. It's a hefty reward for having fun.

Touring isn't difficult or strenuous. Preparation and some planning are essential, but you're simply cycling while carrying on your bike the necessities you'll need that night and the next day, and maybe for the next night and day. Repeat that as often as you need to for longer trips.

Since touring involves more than just you and your cycling equipment, I'll describe three basic touring categories (or approaches to touring) and then divide a major portion of this chapter into three main sections— Equipment for Touring, Making Your Bike Tour-Ready, and Merging the Bike with the Gear. Those three sections on equipment, supplies, and preparation will be followed by a fourth, devoted to your first tour. Preparation is important when choosing and using equipment, so get the whole picture before buying anything. You can easily compare bicycle touring to backpacking. Sometimes touring's even referred to as "bikepacking."

Let's briefly examine three basic types of trips. I refer to them as the organized tour, the planned tour, and the casual, or happy-go-lucky tour.

Organized tours are managed as businesses. You show up and they give you a bike and tell you every turn and pedal stroke you'll make for the next four days and seven hours. Planned tours are those you conduct yourself by deciding ahead of time where you'll finish each day and at what time. Happy-go-lucky tours are just what the name implies. You say to yourself,

By the late 1920s and early 1930s, magazine writers and illustrators were depicting the popularity of bicycle camping. Its popularity has continued to grow ever since, and is far easier and more comfortable today, thanks to lightweight synthetic materials.

Resting at roadside during an overnight tour, Nancy Hofmann peels an orange—a very nutritious thirst-quencher—in one long strip. She has learned how to travel light, and what you see on the bike is all she'd need to tour for as long as she wanted.

"Sometime, probably Thursday, I'll leave home and head west, maybe end up in Ohio or British Columbia, and come home when I'm ready."

Organized tours are package deals that offer a variety of routes, distances, and challenges in the company of a group. Often breakfasts and suppers are included. A "sag wagon"—a van with a repair crew—shows up at regular intervals along the course, and the tour company buses your gear to the next night's stop. Often a group leader rides along to make sure all the riders arrive at the destination. Many of these tours are reasonably priced. Typically, the group of cyclists is small, perhaps numbering no more than twenty.

You can find these group tours advertised in bicycling magazines, or ask about them at your local bike shop. You may even consult a travel guide. Shop around; many groups can provide tours and show you sights unavailable on maps, and they can help you get a feel for more of the local culture than just the tourist traps. (Tourist traps are readily locatable on any map—there's no need to pay anyone to show those to you.) Be sure to inquire about the terrain, clothing you should bring, preparation, etc.

Vacationers often rack their bikes on the family car. On organized group tours, you can take your own bike or rent one from the tour company. The tour operator transports the bicycles to the starting point.

Organized tours attract the widest range of riders, as I discovered for myself. I met an organized tour group during a happy-go-lucky tour of my own down the coast of Maine. Frank was one of the riders, quite an interesting man of about sixty. An art teacher in Rhode Island, he didn't own a car, and he had cycled through Italy and France alone. He enjoyed his solo excursions, but also relished the companionship that group tours offer. On the same trip was Sondra. Sondra lived in Florida, and seldom left. Her cycling experience consisted of riding around her neighborhood regularly for two weeks before the trip. She was the cautious sort, but determined to "find some adventure." Frank brought his bike; Sondra rented one from the tour people.

I tailored my happy-to-lucky tour to meet them every other day. Frank enjoyed the company. Sondra tasted the adventure she sought. I savored both. See? Touring is versatile, too—three riders, three goals, one activity.

Planned tours offer more independence and flexibility, demand more responsibility, and require more planning than organized tours. However, the flexibility occurs only at the planning stage; the tour itself is necessarily tainted by regimentation. It's planned like a family vacation— you know when you'll leave, what route to take, the predicted weather, how long you'll be riding that day, and where you'll sleep that night. It's not difficult, just regimented. The more you plan (and stick to the plan), the more regimented it is. However, confidence comes easily because you always know what should happen next. And once you've developed sufficient confidence, you do have the option of modifying or abandoning the plan at some point during the trip.

Happy-go-lucky tours are my favorite. If you can learn to handle this type comfortably, you can manage the other two easily, so we'll concentrate on happy-go-lucky touring for the rest of the chapter. You plan very little, and just "wing it," through fluid pedal strokes, with warm winds at your back, and sometimes cool rain on your face.

Planning so little demands preparing for anything you're likely to encounter. This isn't as overwhelming as it may sound. Chances are you're just going to venture around some roads in your state or a neighboring state, or perhaps on a trail in the woods, and spend the night wherever you wind up. That's the intriguing part—you're not going home, so you prepare to spend the night anywhere.

To help you prepare and accumulate the equipment you'll need, consider this scenario: You're preparing Saturday's breakfast. You crack

A joy of happy-go-lucky touring is that there are few rules or restrictions. Kathy selected a Cape Cod campground as her "home-point" and cycled around the Cape on day trips. Do it that way and you can leave your gear at the campground, so there's no bother with setting up and taking down equipment. Also, riding an unloaded bike can be a welcome break.

Here's a small, typical assortment of survival necessities. At the top are a down sleeping bag in its stuff sack and a toiletries kit. Next to the loaf of bread (included in the picture for size comparison only) are stuff sacks in three sizes. The largest (5x11 inches) is big enough to hold the sleeping bag. At bottom are a cooking kit (with compact stove inside) and collapsible lantern.

open an egg and *whoosh!*—a genie appears, turban on his head, scarab on the turban, his arms folded across his chest, just like in the cartoons. He glares down at you and booms, "You must spend tonight in the woods alone. I'll give you anything you want, as long as you can carry it all in one large brown paper grocery bag. I'll be back in ten minutes, and then you must tell me what you want to take with you." He disappears in a purple haze. The smoke clears, and a brown paper grocery bag lies at your feet. You gaze at the bag for a helpless moment, then check your watch and run to your nightstand to get *The Cyclist's Bible*. "It's in here somewhere," you mutter, and flip to...

EQUIPMENT FOR TOURING

Racks and Panniers

Carry your gear in panniers, in a small handlebar bag, and on a rear rack. (If your tent, sleeping bag, stove, and mess kit can be packed in a very small space, perhaps you can forego the rear rack.) Panniers are simply gear bags that mount on racks, which mount to your bike frame. (The mounting of racks will be covered later in this chapter, in the section on making your bike tour-ready.) I use and recommend a pair of panniers of about 1,500 cubic inches total volume, or about the size of a large paper grocery bag. You can mount them on a front or rear rack, and they're large enough for the necessities and a few small luxuries. They're the only panniers I've ever had, and they've accompanied me on overnight trips, planned trips, and two-week, thousand-mile happy-go-lucky tours. Panniers that are 2,500 cubic inches in volume are available, but they can only be mounted on the rear rack. You may need that extra 1,000 cubic inches for extended touring, but otherwise you're carrying too much.

Panniers should have an external compression strap, or cinch strap. This strap encircles the pannier, the way a belt encircles you. Since your pannier isn't always stuffed, tightening the strap prevents your gear from moving and makes the bike more predictable. Tightened cinch straps keep your gear as stable as possible even when the pannier is full.

A small to mid-sized handlebar bag—no larger than 400 cubic inches—is great for carrying road food, a camera, light jacket, wallet—anything you need without digging for it. Don't get too large a bag, though; too much weight high on your bike makes handling more sluggish and less predictable. Get the plastic map pouch when you buy the handlebar bag—its convenience is worth its weight in gold.

An excellent way to prepare for a trip is to visualize it, event by event. Make the trip mentally (in abbreviated form, of course), and mentally camp out for the night. Visualizing what you'll be doing and how you'll spend the night is an ideal way to help determine your requirements. Imagine what you'll encounter when you're standing in the woods and it's dark; your bike's by your side; you're hungry, tired, and slapping mosquitoes. The heavy, dank air tells you it may rain. This environment—woods, heavy, dank air, night—and these feelings of hunger, fatigue, and itching suggest the ingredients you'll need to spend the night comfortably.

Shelter

You need shelter to keep you dry and keep out bugs. It provides an "inside," where you go for protection and privacy. The tent must also be lightweight (preferably under 5 pounds), pack small, and be easy to erect.

Long gone are heavy, musty-smelling, canvas tents that always had a hole in the wall and an earwig inside. Now tents are made from rip-stop nylon, and it's easy to find one that's suitable in size and weight for bicycle touring.

My first tent was a two-man nylon pup-tent that I bought for $20 at KMart. It weighed 3 1/2 pounds, packed to about 5 by 17 inches, and stayed upright and leakproof through heavy thunderstorms. It provided an excellent introduction to bicycle touring, and my brother uses it today.

These attributes couldn't compensate for its single-walled construction, though. This means the walls are coated to be waterproof. (The floors of all tents are waterproof.) When I was alone, the tent was fine, even during humid Pennsylvania summers. But in the morning, after two people slept in it, the tent walls looked like a freshly waxed car hood after a rain—a flat surface with beads of water all over it. Bodies give off moisture—it all but "rains" in the tent, and your body is the cloud. Unless the moisture is carried away by moving air, it finds tent walls an ideal place to accumulate.

Double-walled tents have porous walls, so moisture passes through them. A waterproof rain fly is attached a few inches outside the tent walls

A typical two-person, lightweight, double-walled tent, shown without its rainfly and with the rainfly in place.

The rainfly is separated from the tent wall by a few inches, letting air circulate to remove any moisture given off by the bodies of occupants.

to ward off rain. The gap between the fly and the tent wall lets moving air carry away the moisture given off by your body. What the air doesn't remove collects on the inside of the fly, but there's still a barrier of air between the condensation and the tent wall, so you stay dry.

Double-walled tents can be a pound heavier, but it's a pound worth carrying—you'll be far more comfortable in the long run. Double-walled tents also cost more, but aren't prohibitively expensive (although you'll never find one for near $20). Their overall construction is generally of higher quality than that of single-walls, too.

Double-walled tents can be easier to erect, and some are free-standing, so you don't have to stake them. But they should be staked once erected—they can catch wind, like sails. I've seen them blow away, even

A packed tent is the bulkiest item you're likely to tote. It won't fit into a bread box, but it doesn't miss by much. This one is a two-person tent with rainfly, and it weighs about 4 pounds.

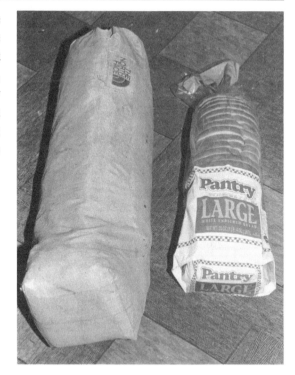

when filled with gear; it's not pretty. Also, dry your tent before packing it; moisture can lead to mildew, which will eventually destroy your tent.

Try this with a free-standing tent. Erect your tent and put it where you want it. Then, before you secure it with stakes, lie inside on your back, in the same way you'll sleep that night. Move from one side of the tent to the other, on your back. If nothing pokes you in the back all the way across, you should have a comfortable sleep.

Sleeping Bag

A sleeping bag must keep you warm and, like all backpacking equipment, should compress tightly so you can pack it small. The argument about whether down or synthetics is the better insulator has continued for years. The fact is that, ounce for ounce, down is the better insulator and compresses smaller, but it's useless when wet and is more expensive. Synthetic insulators are the opposite—they continue to insulate when wet, and are less expensive, but not as warm and won't pack as tightly. For touring in warm weather, you can choose a synthetically insulated bag that will compress tightly enough and will also keep you cozy.

Use the minimum temperature rating to narrow your choices. If you intend to tour only in warm weather, a bag with a minimum temperature rating of 40 degrees Fahrenheit should be sufficient. Three-season touring may demand a rating of 20 degrees. Remember that a warmer bag requires more space and more money.

Compare total weights, not fill weights. The fill weight is the weight of the insulation; the total weight is the weight of the insulation and shell combined, or the whole bag.

The shape and size matter, too. A mummy bag (one that tapers toward the foot) is warmer and packs smaller than a rectangular bag, but may feel confining, especially if you have a large frame. I'm not a big guy (6 feet, 170 pounds) and I have a mummy bag, but my next one may be rectangular. I'd prefer that little extra space, and my bag's low temperature rating (20 degrees Fahrenheit) is only 5 degrees lower than its rectangular counterpart's. Many bags are available in regular and long lengths; be sure to buy one to accommodate your height.

Consider using a sleeping pad with your sleeping bag. It will be a barrier between you and the damp ground, thus keeping you warmer. Various types are available, but most often I use a thin piece of packing foam. It doesn't cushion, but it provides a moisture-proof barrier between the cold ground and me. It packs small, and I keep it in my tent bag. Once, in late fall, I made a "nest" from fallen leaves and erected my tent on it. It provided more than cushion—it, too, got me off the ground, but I also used my packing foam under my sleeping bag.

Air mattresses are too heavy and inconvenient for cycle touring. I brought an air mattress on my first longer-than-overnight tour. When I tried to pack it after the first use, I couldn't get all the air out, and thus couldn't compress it enough to pack it properly. I tried to give it away (I was staying in a state park) but nobody wanted it.

Stoves and Food

Use a small backpacking stove for cooking in the woods. Open fires aren't permitted in many areas and can be extremely dangerous when the forest or grass is dry, or on a windy day when there's nothing to barricade your fire

Nancy Hofmann sets up the stove to cook dinner. Both the stove and eating utensils nest inside the cook kit. You can carry the fuel bottle in a third water-bottle cage. The author mounts his under the down tube, near the bottom bracket housing.

with. Some stoves now are so small they'll fit into your mess kit and weigh well under a pound. They burn white gas (Coleman fuel); the more expensive stoves will burn nearly any widely available fuel, including kerosene and leaded or unleaded gasoline. However, using the wrong fuel can be dangerous. Follow the manufacturer's directions when choosing a fuel.

Cycle touring has a major benefit over backpacking in that you don't have to carry food with you—you can buy food a few miles before you're done riding for the day, or set up camp and then either buy food or cycle to a restaurant. Of course, if you're touring on the trail, you'll have to carry your own easy-to-prepare food, such as pasta. You can always buy dehydrated and freeze-dried foods, but that gets expensive. For variety, consult a trail recipe and menu book.

Clothing

I use the same clothing for trips as for regular cycling (see Chapter 3). Cycling clothing compresses easily and dries quickly when wet. For cooler weather, polypropylene insulates well, wet or dry, uses a modicum of space, and also dries quickly. It's convenient to choose clothing that you can wash when you're done riding for the day, hang it, and have it dry the next morning.

Don't spend a lot of money on backpacking equipment to bicycle tour until you know for certain that you'll stay interested in it. You'll have to buy racks, panniers, and the handlebar bag, but consider renting or borrowing backpacking equipment, especially the big-ticket items—tents, sleeping bags, and stoves. Many camping supply stores rent equipment.

You can gather a lot of information from catalogs and advertisements. They're an easy way to compare prices and features. But be wary of prices and features that are too good to be true. For example, an otherwise reputable bicycle-sales catalog once advertised a tent that seemed unbelievably light. It was. The eye-catching weight was given without considering the weight of the rainfly. It's like saying, "I'm a few pounds overweight, Madge, but if I don't count my arms—." There's no excuse for this. Luckily, this practice is not a rule—most ads and catalogs are reliable.

MAKING YOUR BIKE TOUR-READY

When your bicycle and survival necessities are properly put together, you have a well-equipped vehicle that's ready to carry you many miles from home and will enable you to spend the night wherever you may wind up. Unless you've definitely decided you're going to do major-league touring, you may not want to spend the money for a genuine touring bike, but that's not a problem. Luckily, almost any bike can be made suitable for touring. Only a true racing bike isn't tour-capable.

A mountain bike can be easily adapted to become a touring bike. The mountain bike, like the touring bike, is designed to soak up bumps and provide stable travel. It has to—negotiating roots and rocks on unpredictable trails demands more stability than most potholes ever will. A mountain bike has the extra low gears that are so beneficial for touring, too. Most mountain bikes have cantilever brakes—and these mechanically efficient brakes are great at stopping a loaded bike. They feel as if they could stop a tractor-trailer. For a short tour, no modifications are really needed. Longer tours may merit the addition of road-touring tires, drop handlebars, and toe clips to improve comfort and efficiency.

Many ordinary road bikes will do just fine, also. I adapted my first serious bike to be my touring bike. Nearly fourteen years old now, it cost

Nearly any bike can be made tour-ready. This entry-level bicycle has a basic tour setup. The sleeping bag is lashed to the rear rack, atop the tent.

Long-distance bicycle touring has a long history. In 1895, George T. Loher used this type of "modern" bike (very trim for its era) to travel from San Francisco to New York City.

For Al Sagazio's happy-go-lucky West Virginia tour, he added larger rear cogs to prepare for five-mile climbs. A triple crankset would have been more effective, but also more expensive.

well under $300 when new, and it still reliably takes me on tours ranging from forty-mile overnighters to a thousand miles in two weeks. I added racks to carry my panniers, and lower gears to climb West Virginia's hills, but it's still a 12-speed.

Racks

Regardless of what bike you're going to use, you'll need racks to hold the panniers that carry your gear. Basically, there are three types of racks—two types mount on the front of the bike, and the classic rear rack, of course, mounts on the back. Racks mount to the threaded eyelets on the fork, chain stays, and seat stays. Panniers hook on the top and bottom of a rack, with the bottom hook attached to an adjustable cord so you can apply tension to keep the pannier motionless.

We've all seen the classic rear rack—it looks like a simple wire shelf over your back tire (not the rack with the spring clip on it). You can hang

The classic rear rack is nearly universal on touring bikes. You can load a tent and sleeping bag on top and hang panniers along the sides.

The Blackburn Lowrider front rack holds the panniers low, centered on the front hub. This greatly improves a bike's handling and eases climbing.

panniers on it, and lay a tent or sleeping bag on top of it. I weave a bungee-cord back and forth across the top of my rear rack to prevent my tent from scraping the back tire, but some rear racks have a shelf built in. This shelf also helps keep dirt and mud off gear carried on the rack. I use two additional bungee cords to hold my tent on top of the rack.

The standard front rack is a mirror image of the rear rack. However, this rack has largely been supplanted (for touring) by the Blackburn Company's "Lowrider" front rack. It positions your panniers low, centered on the front hub. Maneuvering and climbing with this unorthodox-looking setup is easier than with your panniers mounted on the rear rack. I toured for several years using only the Lowrider front rack. I added a rear rack when I bought my double-walled tent, which packs slightly larger than my old single-walled tent. The only disadvantage of the Lowrider is that it has no shelf, although it can be mounted in

Front and rear racks are easily installed on a bike by means of threaded eyelets on the front fork and at the top and bottom of the rear seat stays. The threaded eyelet is the little circle near the center of this photo, brazed onto the frame.

conjunction with a standard Blackburn front rack. However, unless you're going to be touring for years at a time, I doubt you'll really need that front shelf.

LOADING YOUR BIKE

Pack your gear into stuff sacks and hook your panniers onto the racks. Stuff sacks are nylon bags with a drawstring at the top, suitable for organizing your gear. They come in various sizes and colors, so you can pack systematically, and they're available wherever backpacking equipment is sold.

Pack the heaviest items at the bottom and to the inside of your panniers, closest to the rack. Lighter, smaller items go on top, or in small external pockets if your panniers have them. Then mount the panniers firmly to the rack, and finally, tighten the compression strap. That's all there is to it; you're ready for your trial run. After your first couple of trips, trial runs probably won't be necessary. You'll be surprised at how quickly you become adept at packing and balancing your loads.

Find an area away from any traffic, obstacles, and distractions. (A mall's parking lot early on Sunday morning may be adequate.) Walk the bike a few yards and steer it. It will, of course, feel heavier than usual. Riding the bike will feel the same way—a little heavy, but certainly manageable. You won't stop as quickly, but with a little practice, riding a loaded touring bike will soon be as natural as riding your unloaded bike. Your bike is wider now, so be careful, especially when cycling alongside parked cars. It also won't respond as quickly, so you must look a little farther ahead (or ride slower) to buy the extra time you may need to react.

Maps

I usually tour by following the smallest, grayest lines on an AAA road map. Instead of connecting route numbers, I travel from town to town by following the arrow on the green roadsigns. You've seen them—"Erwinsville 4" (then a right arrow), "LaValle 10" (then an up arrow, meaning straight ahead). AAA road maps give you the big picture and are great for lengthy road tours. They also give the distance between towns right on the line that connects those towns, so you can tell the real scale, not just one inch equals five miles. Real scale considers terrain. If you have a scale of one inch equals

This advertising poster of the mid-1880s promoted an American book of fictionalized cycling adventures—long-distance bike touring.

five miles, and a one-inch line, you can bet the actual distance is five miles. If there's a big hill in the way, one inch may equal ten miles. AAA maps give you the real distances, are widely available, and they're consistent.

Very detailed maps are available from an organization called Bikecentennial. The charge is reasonable for the maps, and they're printed in a sturdy little booklet. For more information, see Appendix III.

Off-road riding demands a different kind of map. State and national parks with trails for riding almost always have free maps at the ranger stations. Guidebooks with trails specific to local areas are in great demand, and more are being published.

Chambers of commerce in many areas may also have information and will help you obtain maps for both on- and off-road riding.

YOUR FIRST TOUR

Although this book provides the information and advice you need for touring by the seat of your pants, it's a good idea to make your first tour an organized or planned tour.

In the introduction, I emphasized that touring is merely a true extension of casual riding. No one will laugh or poke fun at you if you decide not to camp. I often mix camping with motels during a tour—each approach offers the chance to get away from the other, and each has obvious attractions.

Choose a first-tour destination close to home, at a distance you feel comfortable riding in a day. Remember, you'll be riding home the next day, so make sure you can ride that distance two days in a row. Also, if you're riding with a companion, consider the differences in your riding styles, endurance, enthusiasm, and physical condition. One of you may have followed all the fitness and conditioning advice in Chapter 6 while the other watched TV and gained weight. Bear in mind that one person (as well as one bike) may be a better road machine than the other.

This point may be made most persuasively with an example. Let's say I can ride sixty miles in four hours, but that's as long as I can comfortably stay on the bike. My partner can also ride sixty miles, but needs five hours. At least one of us, and probably both, will be miserable before the

Nearly ready to hop on and roam, Nancy has packed the heavy items into the bottom inner portion of her panniers, loaded her handlebar bag and rear rack, and is now tightening the cinch straps.

ride is over. It's a problem of time, not speed. Make sure all the riders on a trip can ride for as long as is required on any given day.

Call ahead to the motel or campground you've chosen and tell them you'll be arriving by bicycle; saying you're traveling by "bike," or that you're "a biker," may unfortunately elicit an unfair prejudice against motorcycling, an image of chains and knives, studded leather jackets, and bizarre tattoos.

On the night before my first tour, I felt apprehensive, but it was the kind of apprehension you feel from excitement, not fear. I calmed myself by mentally touring—not mile by mile, but event by event. This is a

On a happy-go-lucky tour, there's always time for a rest whether it's needed or merely desired. This cyclist enjoys time out overlooking a beautiful lake in New Hampshire. That's what touring is all about.

valuable technique that I strongly recommend, and I'll show you how by taking you on a mental tour.

Since you're about to accomplish a goal, view the end first, then the means to achieve it, and, finally, all the little details that get the job done.

I said we'll tour event by event, so now imagine riding, drinking, snacking or lunching, unpacking at your destination, checking in at a motel or setting up camp, washing, eating dinner, sleeping, waking, and anything else you may have to do. You'll see just where you'll use each item of your survival gear. You'll also ensure that you don't bring too much or too little, or the wrong thing. (I get annoyed when I return from a trip and realize I haven't used something. Repair tools are an exception; I get annoyed when I do have to use those.)

As you acknowledge an item, put it in front of you so it's ready to pack, Write it down, too, and you'll have a permanent record of what you took. At the end of the imaginary ride, you can delete what you didn't use so you won't waste time or space with it when you actually tour. This isn't foolproof, but it will eliminate most if not all superfluous items. Then, if you do pack a useless item or two on your actual tour, you'll know to leave it home next time.

Relax now, and imagine the morning of your first tour. The only gear you're now using is the clothing you're wearing for that day's ride. Start at your head, then proceed down from your helmet and out from the inside layer. You're wearing your helmet, sunglasses, shirt, jacket, gloves, shorts or tights, socks, and shoes. Is something missing? Go to the bottom drawer of your dresser and get it.

Now you begin to ride. After a few miles, you get thirsty, so you drink from your water bottle. You need directions, so you consult your map. You get hungry, and you eat a banana. You get a flat tire, so you get your tool kit and you get annoyed. A doe and two fawns drink from a creek, so you get your camera.

Stop your imaginary tour now and notice what you put in front of you—water bottle, map, road food, tool kit, and camera. (Leave your temper at home.) These items don't act independently or alone; they have components. Gather the components and assemble what you can. For example, fill the water bottle; slip your map into the little plastic case that's worth its weight in gold, snap it to the handlebar bag, and mount the handlebar bag to the handlebars; make sure your camera has film in it. Make sure you've packed extra rolls of film.

Now you arrive at your imaginary destination. Let's assume you've decided on camping instead of moteling. It's just a matter of using the survival gear you already know how to use. What will you do first? Set up your tent? All right, put it in front of you. Now you want to wash, and since many campgrounds have coin-activated showers, imagine putting the coins in the slot, and washing. (Did you bring along coins? You can't always get change for a $5 bill.) Put the coins, soap, shampoo, towel, a change of clothing, toothbrush, and toothpaste in front of you. Imagine your supper, and get your sustenance supplies. It might be chilly tonight—add your jacket and pants. A mosquito bit you—slap it and get the insect repellent. You like to read before sleeping, so get your book and light source, and your sleeping bag.

What will you wear the next morning? What will you have for breakfast? Where will you ride today? Will it rain? Answer these questions in the same manner, by envisioning the act and putting the item in front of you.

One cautionary note: It's easy to become lazy with this exercise after you've toured a few times. Steps become routine and taken for granted. That's one advantage of having a list (such as the sample list at the end of this chapter), but you have to use it. Don't use your list the way I use calendars—I write down everything on my calendar, but I only look at the calendar when I'm writing something on it. I've never forgotten anything major on a tour, but I did forget matches once. They should have been with my cooking kit. Had I been touring in the woods, my hunger could have radically altered my appreciation of touring that night. It isn't pleasant to go hungry after a day's riding, so don't let yourself get lazy with this mental exercise. Take the time to go through each step, or consult your list to the letter.

Extended tours, or those lasting more than one night, are less predictable than shorter ones. Weather and wind become less predictable, terrain is less familiar, your overall physical and mental state are less predictable (though not severely except in rare cases), and sometimes a combination of the above can create obstacles rather than pleasures. Even when these conditions are predictable, you're covering more ground, so the chances of variation are greater. You just have to be more prepared. Also, since you're traveling for a longer time, more obstacles can arise.

One point bears repeating, especially when planning an extended tour. If

Here's Al Sagazio, his Lowriders loaded, cycling easily at his own pace. Long hours on the road are more comfortable and pleasant if you've taken the time and forethought to pack your panniers so that the bike is well balanced.

you're traveling with companions, it's vitally important to consider your partners' riding styles. The slowest member of your group will determine how long you'll ride each day. This is especially important on extended tours.

Day one of an extended tour is usually sunny and 70 degrees, calm, and flat. Nobody knows why; it just works that way. But day two can be windy and rainy and chilly and hilly. You must prepare for all of this, while using a minimal amount of space.

I got burned once by taking the weather and myself for granted. What I thought was a 300-mile trip turned into 400, which wouldn't have been too bad had I not been ambitiously trying to complete the trip in three days.

Also, eastern Pennsylvania summers seldom get much below 60 degrees at night, so I thought a tee-shirt and two mesh shirts would be appropriate to get me to West Virginia in the middle of August. They were indeed appropriate—except when I woke up after spending the night on a towpath.

Survival Essentials

Cycling Apparel
  helmet
  shirt
  shorts
  socks
  shoes
  gloves
  sunglasses
Bike Gear
  water bottle
  frame pump
  seat pack
  tool kit
  map
  panniers, each lined
    with a plastic bag
  handlebar bag
Road Food
Money
Camera with Film
Tent, Sleeping Bag and
  Sleeping Pad
Toiletries, etc.
  coins
  soap
  shampoo
  towel
  toothbrush
  toothpaste

  comb or brush
  contact-lens equipment
    (if applicable)
  deodorant
  toilet paper
  flashlight
  insect repellent
Stove and Cooking Gear
  fuel bottle
  mess kit
  utensils (spoon, fork, etc.)
  cup
  matches
Clothing
  underwear
  socks
  shirt
  shorts or long pants
  shoes (if you're not using
    touring shoes)
  jacket
  cool-weather clothing
    (if required)
Miscellaneous
  watch
  wallet
  money
  candle

Towpaths are banks that run parallel to canals. Men and mules walked these paths when towing canalboats, and they're often tree-covered and damp. Inside my sleeping bag I was warm. But when I got out I froze. When I reached town an hour later, the bank thermometer read 49 degrees. A little later that day, I spoke with a man who showed me where frost had killed his flowers. He worked a night shift, and when he came home at two in the morning his thermometer read 28 degrees—28 degrees in August! Weather's fickle, and especially so in the mountains.

I learned my lesson, and it summed up touring preparation well. Just be prepared for things somewhat outside the boundaries of the usual. Then let go. You're going to have fun.

Many camping books and magazine articles include packing lists, and they're extremely useful—but only as general guidelines. What's essential for me (I like photography and I read myself to sleep) may be superfluous to you. On the other hand, a diary and pencil or pen—or maybe knitting materials—may be essential to you and useless to me. The same is true of medications, of course. You'll find a list of suggested essentials below. You'll be wise to make a copy of it, put it in front of you as you make your mental tour, and add or cross off items as needed.

8

Real Mountain Biking

"Mountain biking." What in the world does it really mean? Today, many little kid who routinely puts his pants on backward may own a mountain bike, or something he thinks is a mountain bike, or something touted by the manufacturer (or department store) as a mountain bike. But is it? What mountain biking really means is bicycling over rocks and through mud and up steep, grassy hills, or anywhere else you want to go.

Although the mountain bike evolved to grab the mass market, there are serious mountain bikes being pounded by serious riders. These riders rightfully think there's nothing strange about bicycling up the side of a steep mountain, where no one would consider building a ski slope, just so they can race down it, dodging trees, hopping rocks, and spraying mud. They often get together for "rallies," races, and other competitions.

But trail riding isn't only for the competitive. In one respect, trail riding is just like road riding—you choose the route to match your level of experience and ability. When you feel confident riding along the grassy paths, move on to dirt. Eventually you'll have the confidence to tackle the rocks and roots. If you want to try the rough stuff on your first time out, go ahead—common sense should get you through the bulk of it, and you can walk your bike if the going gets too tough.

However, at whatever level you ride, let someone know where you plan to do it on a given day. If you're out there alone and have an accident, hours or days may pass before someone wanders by that area.

Mountain bikes, or all-terrain bikes (ATBs), gained popularity in the mid-'80s when the country got caught up in a fitness craze. This wasn't a bad thing—we became aware that physical fitness and a good basic diet are necessities for a healthy life. Mountain bikes, with their upright handlebars,

Now *this* is mountain biking—narrow, unpaved trails, backwoods, plenty of bumps, but not a road sign, yellow line, or car in sight!

A mountain biker rides a mountain crest. There are few places an ATB can't navigate. You can achieve new heights— let yourself go!

It's common practice for a club or group of friends to meet at a designated spot and hit the trail. Usually it takes only a few minutes for everyone to get their bikes set up. Some riders may even cycle to the rendezvous. The Genesis Bicycles staff organized this Pennsylvania mountain-bike outing, and welcomed friends and customers.

A mountain-bike tire is so wide it may not fit in the tray of some popular roof-rack auto carriers, but you can still car-top your bike safely and securely. It just takes a bit of ingenuity. Here, a toe strap holds the wheel to the tray.

thick tires, and reasonable seats, attracted potential cyclists who wouldn't ordinarily have considered going anywhere by pedal power. These bicycles look friendly and inviting, not competitive like those skinny bikes with their skinny tires and skinny seats and weird, contorted handlebars that seemingly aren't good for anything except going fast.

That's largely how the mountain bike became popular—a "relaxed" general public wanted an easy way to get in shape, or at least become part of the fitness trend, and have fun while doing it. The mountain bike did more than just get people to ride. It stimulated—jump-started, actually—a slowly fading bicycle market to become stronger than ever, no doubt saving a few businesses and starting many more.

I greet this last development with mixed emotions. I-the-Purist feel too many people have bought mountain bikes because they were the "in"

Trail riding can (and usually does) have an air of casualness. These riders have very diverse levels of experience, but everyone was once a slowpoke so no one gets impatient. They're resting and chatting while waiting at the top of a tough hill for their companions.

Hand guards can be a blessing when briars, twigs, or brush line your way.

thing to have, not because they were the best choice for their purpose. Most mountain bikes will never touch a trail, so their riders would probably derive more benefit and enjoyment from a bike meant to be ridden on the road. But I'd be a fool and a hypocrite to criticize someone for buying a mountain bike, loving every minute of road riding on it, and deriving mental and physical benefits from doing just that.

If you have a mountain bike, enjoy it. Its beauty is that you can ride it wherever you legally please—that's what it's designed for. If you're shopping for a bike, though, one of this book's strong messages is the advantage of choosing a model that's most practical for the type of riding you intend to do. Now, let's get to the fun of off-road bicycling.

Ron was always asking me when I was going to try some "real" cycling. By that he meant riding through the woods on a trail that was never the same twice. It would change with a rain, and change again after the mud hardened. If the wind blew, it'd change again. And if the air was still, the trail would change anyway. The change of seasons changed the paths; so did the sun's rise and set.

Ron had a new mountain bike, so I borrowed his old one, and off we went—Ron, Pauline (his fiancee), and I. We dawdled along a quiet road, then pedaled side-by-side-by-side along a manicured strip of meadow someone had planted in the middle of the woods. Not too different from road riding so far, I thought; it's a little harder to pedal because of the soft terrain, fat tires, upright handlebar position, and heavier bike, but gearing down takes care of that.

Ten minutes later, Ron said, "Turn left up there."

I looked up, but saw nothing different from what I had seen for the last mile. "Just past the oak tree and briar bush," he clarified. I must have given him my best confused-puppy look, because then he said, "See that big rock on the right?"

I nodded.

"About thirty feet beyond that, but on the left."

Okay, I nodded again, trying to be convincing by nodding my whole torso, although I still didn't know where he was talking about. I dropped back a few feet, just to be safe. Of course, by that time, we were turning left.

We turned and rode single file for about a hundred feet. Then I saw the kind of path Ron had mentioned when he goaded me into mountain biking—a typical path you'd find in the woods. It had pockmarks and aberrations—if you were walking, you'd find a sturdy stick to use as a third leg—and it was only about 18 inches wide. A single track, they call it. Riding on this trail would be worse than any potholed road. I was about to have my first mountain-biking lesson.

NAVIGATING THE TRAIL

Often there's no way you can avoid the obstacles on a path. There's a rock on the left side of the trail and a big root on the other side, 5 feet beyond it, and the path is only 18 inches wide. Although it may at first seem like a pain in the neck, it's a big part of the challenge—and the fun.

The line of travel with the fewest bumps is usually the easiest to negotiate. Determine the path you're going to take, fix it in your mind, and make it happen. Indecisiveness has lost World Series games, caused traffic accidents, and dropped major accounts. At first you'll probably just come to a stop. Learn from this and you'll become a better rider.

Sometimes you can't go around obstacles and must go over them. Learn to pull your front wheel up, over the top of these hurdles, like "pulling a wheelie" when you were a kid, then pedaling your back wheel over as you transfer your weight forward. With more practice and

For a skillful mountain biker like Dean Jones, a fallen tree merely provides fun and variety. Just pull up on the handlebar to "jump" the front wheel, and pedal the back wheel right over it. This kind of obstacle would force a road-bike rider to dismount and lift the bicycle over.

This lever permits quick adjustment of the seat height. For challenging descents, try lowering your seat an inch or more to achieve extra control.

experience, you can "bunny hop" your bike—pulling up on the handlebars while "jumping" from your pedals. Concentrate on where you'll come down before you go up. Also, be aware of your handlebar's position—you're immediately going in that direction when you land.

Plenty of trails will require walking around or over obstacles. Perhaps the trail is too rocky or broken, or the mud is so soft it bogs you down. You have no choice but to get off the bike and walk. That's part of the adventure and completeness of mountain biking.

RIDE READY

If the downhill path is bumpy and full of obstacles, you'll probably stand on the pedals. You're moving faster now, so you must be ready to turn quickly, stop short, and soak up bumps, even if you have a shock absorber on your bike.

When you stand on the pedals, keep your rear end low, but off the seat. Ride with your knees bent and your weight centered over the balls of your feet, as if you were skiing, especially when you're going down a bumpy hill. There's not a single activity that's done best or safest with your knees locked. Bent knees act as shock absorbers to keep the jolt from getting to your body. Bending also allows you to react quicker, whether you're

These extensions of the handlebar make climbing easier. Changing your hand positions provides comfort on long rides, too.

maneuvering the bike to avoid a rock or correcting your body angle to maintain your balance.

Athletes in many sports, especially weekend athletes, don't bend their knees enough and aren't as ready to react as they could be. Good form is often sacrificed when you're tired, and it's easy to forget to bend your knees. I play a lot of volleyball, and the more I bend my knees, the more ready I am. The same applies to mountain-bike riding; develop this good habit early through practice and repetition.

BRAKING

On a smooth, flat trail, you stop your ATB just as you would stop your road bike—using both brakes, and applying pressure evenly and simultaneously (see Chapter 4). But on steep descents with lots of obstacles and loose dirt, this otherwise proper technique can send you tumbling.

Remember that most of your stopping power comes from your front brake, and your back brake keeps you from pitching over by stopping the transfer of momentum. On a steep hill, your weight will already be high, as if you began pitching over, so the momentum begins "more forward" than it would if you were on flat terrain.

Instead of squeezing both brakes simultaneously, use only your back brake. You'll have more control, and you'll keep it by making sure your front wheel doesn't lock up. Try locking up your rear wheel on short, steep hills and "dragging" your wheel down. If you've been a road cyclist, you're accustomed to using the front and rear brakes together, and you'll tend to do it automatically. Find a local unpaved hill where you can practice mountain-bike braking safely.

SHIFTING GEARS

You have less time to make decisions when you're riding on the trail, so every move and maneuver must be done with more precision, including shifting. I bogged down on the first hill, and I watched Ron ride away steadily. Pauline, a calm and controlled rider, toddled confidently by. I realized why mountain bikes have those super-low gears—you need them to maintain momentum when you're constantly turning and bouncing off obstacles, and to keep your balance. Wooded trails have far more resistance than hard concrete, especially when it has rained the night before.

Shifting gears on the trail must be done with more precision and decisiveness than you need on a smooth road, so manufacturers designed the shift controls on mountain bikes to be accessible without taking your hands from the handlebar. The shift levers are positioned above the brake levers.

Let your legs tell you when to shift, just as in road riding (see Chapter 4). Rocky trails are much less forgiving than roads, and you often can't take your hands off the handlebars without losing control—that's why mountain bikes have shifters on the handlebars, and why manufacturers try to come up with faster and more convenient shifting mechanisms. The crucial point is that you must pay more attention and concentrate more when trail riding—you simply have less time to correct mistakes.

THE ADVANTAGE OF A SHOCK ABSORBER

A shock absorber is often an optional piece of equipment but is now standard on many mountain-bike models and has become extremely popular. On less expensive ATBs, frame quality may be sacrificed for this addition, so shop carefully. A shock absorber does more than provide a

A shock absorber is usually installed on the front, but some advanced bikes have them on the front and rear.

comfortable ride. It helps you to maintain control over very uneven terrain. Since you can't control your bike if your wheel loses contact with the ground, the shock absorber's real job is to keep the wheel in contact with the ground, just as a car's shock does to its wheel.

It works for you like the cushioning spring in a pogo stick. Imagine standing on a step, jumping off, and landing with your legs locked. You'd painfully feel the jolt through your legs, hips, and into your back and neck. But if you're hopping around on a pogo stick, the pogo stick, not you, absorbs that downward energy. The shock absorber does the same thing (except that it's not designed to propel you upward).

Riding a bike with a shock absorber can be a peculiar sensation until you get used to it. Because *it* absorbs the impact instead of you, your bike "gives" when you're expecting a jolt, and you just keep riding. Having a shock absorber can be a tremendous advantage when bustling along a bumpy trail or picking your way down a rocky path. If rough paths excite you, the shock's extra weight is worth carrying

Sometimes you have to stop and pull a small stick from between your spokes, or scrape accumulated mud off your rims. It's just part of the ride.

because it will help and encourage you to make your way over extra-rough terrain.

A shock isn't necessary, but it does help considerably. You can generally cover the same ground without a shock absorber, but you're forced to do it more slowly, and probably for not as long, because you'll get tired sooner. Remember, though, if you measure the difficulty of a trail by whether you need a shock absorber, you can be sure it's rough, even for an experienced mountain biker, so exercise caution.

9

Racing

Throughout history, people have liked to race, and since its introduction, the bicycle has been a popular way to do it. But bicycle racing is often more complex than just crossing the finish line first. It's true that some races are won with brute force, but some are won by accumulating the most points, and still others by riding the greatest distance in the allotted time. Often teams are involved, and most involve tactics and strategy. Smarts and experience will win races when all else is equal.

Almost anyone can race, but you must be realistic about your chances of success without the appropriate talent, training, and desire to excel. Many areas organize road races in which you can participate—check your newspaper, ask at local bike shops, and call bicycling clubs for information.

About fifteen years ago, my doctor told me he had watched the bike races that took place in our town on the previous weekend. They were part of Heritage Day celebration, and he raved about how exciting they were, even though he had no interest in bike racing or even bike riding. As the sport has gained popularity over the years, I've heard the same response from others who have no specific interest in cycling. I'm lucky enough to live near a velodrome (a track on which bike races are run), and many non-riders watch the races with great enthusiasm in the same way they'd watch a ball game. You get caught up in the excitement.

Greater enjoyment comes from an activity when you understand it. Some readers of this book will be eager to compete in certain races (and perhaps a few have already done so). But even if you have no intention of participating, racing is a grand sport to watch. For the uninitiated, however, some of the events can be confusing at first. Since each bike race

142

Illustrator Charles Cox created this 1895 poster to advertise *Bearings,* a popular cycling magazine—and to announce Decoration Day races sponsored by the magazine. Note the dropped handlebars on these racing bikes, which had already evolved along modern lines.

Bike races, whether they're held on the track or the road, often have riders bunched shoulder to shoulder. The cyclists shown here were competing in a 1993 Virginia race. Bike-handling skills must be very good, and the racer must be able to cope with unintentional bumps from other riders. As explained in the text, strategy and tactics can be as important as power.

has different rules and requirements, it pays to be a knowledgeable spectator. Step one is understanding the categories and the rules.

COMPETITION CATEGORIES

The United States Cycling Federation (USCF) is the sanctioning body of amateur road and track racing. The competitors are organized by age and sex, then divided into four categories. Category IV includes beginners and novices. After completing eight "Cat IV" races, you can upgrade to a Category III license. When you place in the top three in three Cat III events, you can move on to the really serious stuff and get your Category II license. Category I races are for the elite: national, international, and Olympic-level racers. For information regarding licensing, including fees ($16 to $32, depending on category), write to:

United States Cycling Federation
1750 E. Boulder St.
Colorado Springs, CO 80909

Also, local bike clubs may be able to provide an application for a license. Incidentally, not all races require participants to be licensed—club races are open to anyone.

ROAD RACING

Any healthy person can participate in amateur road races. In urban areas, from spring to fall, nary a weekend passes without a bike race relatively nearby. They're often sponsored by clubs, and USCF-sanctioned.

The most common race is the criterium. A lap of (usually) less than 2 miles comprises the circuit on which it's run, and the entire race lasts 10 miles or 16 kilometers.

The road race (that's what another specific type of race is called) is run from one point to another or on a 3-mile (maximum) circuit, or a combination of the two. Road races are usually longer than criteriums and have less consistent terrain.

Tandem racing adds to the wide variety of today's cicycling competitions.

Cyclists on the Champs Elysées, the final stage of the Tour de France. The entire nation of France gets caught up in the Tour in a way that dwarfs the enthusiasm generated by the Super Bowl or World Series.

Laurent Fignon leads the Tour de France *peloton* (pack of riders) on the final stage back to Paris. It's an enormous challenge for almost anyone to ride over 150 miles in a day, yet these world-class cyclists *race* that distance against others of their caliber. Remember, too, that the Tour is not a single-day event. This level of intensity prevails for three weeks!

Time trials race each rider against the clock, one rider at a time. The shortest time wins.

Stage races may combine *all* forms of road racing. They're held over several days, each day called a stage. The rider's time for each stage is tallied, and the rider with the lowest total time at the end of the race is the winner.

Stage races are the pinnacle of road racing. The most prestigious are long, grueling races. The Tour de France, a stage race covering 2,200 miles over three weeks, is the granddaddy of them all.

Perhaps nowhere is it more apparent than in the "Tour" that bicycle racing is a team sport. A great cyclist's teammates are akin to a great quarterback's front line. A cycling team is built around one or two stars, those capable of winning it all. As leaders, they must be strong in all aspects of the race. The *domestiques,* or helpers, are excellent racers, but generally lacking in one area or another. However, they're the ones who chase rivals, carry extra food and water, and pull the star along.

VELODROME (TRACK) RACING

If you've never watched a race at a velodrome, you may be confused the first time. With names like kierin, Madison, and miss-and-out, the races are rather hard to figure out without some help. I'm lucky enough to live near the Lehigh County Velodrome in Trexlertown, Pennsylvania (just west of Allentown), and the colorful announcer usually explains what's going on, often referring to riders by their first names, and giving a little history about them.

"Johnny Marshall is trying a breakaway," he'll announce. "And it looks like he's going to get away with it. Johnny's from Indianapolis, and he's been waiting all night to try that."

Track races, like road races, get very crowded, so a competitor's bike-handling skills must be top-notch.

In a team-pursuit race, cyclists try to overtake the riders on the opposing team. These team members will take turns at the front so a fresh rider can "draft" the others. To "draft" is to cleave through air resistance for those to the rear.

Unfortunately, only a handful of velodromes are scattered about the United States, but if you're lucky enough to live near one, I suggest you treat yourself and visit it. I'll briefly describe the most popular track races, beginning with the types that are included in the Olympics.

Individual pursuit. Two riders start on opposite sides of the track and literally chase one another. The rider with the advantage at the end of the distance wins. Men race 4,000 meters; women race 3,000 meters.

Team pursuit. The objective is the same as in the individual pursuit, but four-man teams race. Each team rides single file, with the lead rider rotating to the back of the line after every lap. Three riders on each team must finish.

Kilometer. This is a 1,000-meter race against the clock, one man at a time, from a standing start.

Points race. One of the longer track races, this one requires riders to sprint every fifth lap for points throughout the 50 kilometers. Riders' total points determine their pacing.

Sprint. The last 200 meters of a 1,000-meter race is timed and determines the riders' placement.

World Championship races include the following types:

Tandem sprint. This is the same as the sprint described above, but with two teams on tandems. It's a very strategic race (as are the sprints), and these guys really fly on the final sprint.

Kierin. Nine riders are paced by a motorcycle which moves out of the way for the final lap, on which the riders sprint to the finish.

Motor-paced. Each rider (up to 10 on the track) is paced by a motorcycle in a race that usually lasts for one hour and can average speeds of over 50 miles per hour.

The Madison and miss-and-out are also popular, although they're

A Madison race demands smooth teamwork. Here, the lead rider "hand-slings" his partner into the race.

not included in Olympic or World Championship events. Here's how they're run.

Madison. One rider relays his teammate into the race by "hand-slinging" him. The lead rider reaches back and grabs the hand of a teammate; the trailing rider gains extra speed when the leading rider relays him back into the race. The slinger then rests by slowly circling the track. When he's ready to reenter the race, the process is repeated.

Miss-and-out. The rider in last place at the end of each lap must drop out. When just a few riders are left, they sprint to the finish.

Four specialized kinds of racing bikes are used in these races. (Mountain-bike racing is not included here but will be covered separately.) A specialty bike will let the rider tap his true potential. The four types are the track bike, criterium, road bike, and time-trial bike. These bicycles can be compared to different racing cars. Drag-race cars, stock cars, and Indy cars are built to perform different functions. All are designed to go fast, but on different courses. These bikes are comparable—some are designed for the track, some for shorter races in

The smaller the contact between tire and track or pavement, the less friction there is to slow a bike. A racing bike's tires are therefore extremely narrow to create as little friction as possible.

which the riders cycle as hard as they can for the entire race, and some are a bit more stable and comfortable for races of 150 miles and more.

The track bike is a single-speed, no-frills, bare-bones bike designed to transfer to the road every ounce of energy that the rider exerts on the pedals. It has no freewheeling mechanism in the rear hub, which means you can't stop pedaling. If the back wheel is moving, the chain is moving and the pedals are moving. The bike has no brakes, either, but you can moderately control your speed by resisting the pedals.

Obviously, the track bike has limited practical use anywhere but on a track. But a track bike forces you to pedal in circles, a wonderful exercise that can dramatically improve your pedaling efficiency and style.

You can easily make a practical, road-worthy track bike, and, with the addition of brakes, it will make a great training aid. Nearly any safe frame will do. Replace the back wheel with a track wheel (a wheel with one cog and no freewheel mechanism in the hub) so the drivetrain is direct-drive. Choose the gear most practical for the terrain in your riding area. You can use this bike on the road or on rollers to give you a really smooth pedal motion.

This time-trial racer must fight the wind by himself, with no one ahead to "draft" him, so he makes himself and his bike as aerodynamic as he possibly can. Note the small front wheel and teardrop-shaped helmet.

The criterium bike is like a tight-handling sports car. A criterium race can be short and crowded, so you need a maneuverable bike to get you out of trouble and away from the pack when the moment is right. The head and seat tube angles are steep, so there's no hesitation when you command the bike to turn.

The road bike is similar to the criterium, but a bit more relaxed. Even the small advantages can become monumental after racing for 6 or 7 hours and covering 150 to 170 miles, so a little extra comfort from a softer, less rigid, more stable bike can be a blessing.

The time-trial (TT) bike is made for speed and reduced air resistance. Racers ride alone, so the course is free from obstacles such as other riders, and hence more predictable. But without other riders, "drafting"—reducing air resistance by maneuvering so that the others block the wind—is impossible, so you must cheat the wind yourself. (Even if you manage to catch the rider in front of you, drafting is prohibited during a time-trial.) The effort to make the TT as aerodynamic as possible resulted in an almost modern-art appearance and has earned it the moniker of "funny bike" because of its sloping top tube, tentacle-like handlebars, and aero-everything. And I do mean everything.

Rims, spokes, frame, handlebar, seat post, water bottle, seat(!)—every component on the bike is tapered and rounded so that air flows around with as little resistance as possible. The rider usually shaves his legs and sometimes his arms, wears a skin-tight outfit, and sometimes a swimming cap, all to improve his ability to cut through the wind. The real fanatics even spray their bodies with silicon! (These riders are pros who are sponsored by corporations or hired by teams. Their salary is determined by measuring their performance in hundredths of seconds, so they take any advantage they can get—and all of their competitors do the same.)

MOUNTAIN-BIKE RACING

The National Off-Road Bicycle Association (NORBA) is the mountain-bike riders' equivalent of the USCF, and this organization sanctions mountain-bike races in the United States. The same opportunities apply to mountain-bike racing as to road racing—nearly any healthy person can race, and there are various categories, depending on your age, sex, and experience level.

Mountain-bike riders aren't content to ride just one type of race, either, so they participate in an assortment, from endurance events (similar to running cross-country), to fast, exciting races like the downhill. The following are the most popular races.

Cross-country. This is a criterium on dirt. Such races are usually held on circuits of 2 miles or longer.

Downhill. As the name implies, riders barrel down a course in time-trial fashion, with riders typically starting 30 seconds to 1 minute apart.

Dual slalom. Riders compete on side-by-side courses. As in dual-slalom skiing races, each rider must go through each gate on his own course. They then switch courses and race again. Penalties are assessed for crashing, missing gates, and false starts. The lowest combined time determines the winner.

Hill climb. It's like the motorcycle hill climbs, only this one can be a mass start (all the riders start at the same time) or an individual start. The toughest hill-climb courses can be incredible endurance tests.

Point-to-point. This race is like the cross-country, but raced from one point to another instead of a circuit.

Ultra-endurance. These races are the mountain bike's equivalent of a marathon, and may require riding 75 miles or more, not on the road.

Obviously, some of these races are beyond the capabilities of the average person, but there are races for just about everyone. Often velodromes have amateur leagues, and, if you're not fortunate enough to live near a velodrome (or even if you are), road racing and ATB racing are becoming more and more popular. A friend of mine, who is an avid runner, once urged me to race, but I resisted at first because I didn't want to train. "I don't want to *have* to ride my bike," I said.

"You don't have to train unless you want to," he replied. "I run for the fun of it, because I love to. I don't train, I just run. Racing is still fun, even if I don't win."

So I tried it, and I didn't win. But you know what? He was right—I had a lot of fun. So much fun that I did it again. And again.

In my first road race, I tired halfway through and dropped back from the pack in an effort to conserve energy. This was the biggest mistake I could have made. I should have stayed with the field and let them block the wind for me. As mentioned earlier, this is called drafting, and it's a tactic that can save 20 percent of your energy! Any pack is fast, and fighting the wind resistance all by myself put me even farther back. I never caught the pack in that race, and finished obscurely in the middle of the field.

Events like the World Cup Race for ATBs, held on Mt. St. Anne,
demand exceptional body condition for top performance. Clearly, this
competitor is using more than just his legs in the last stage.

But with each race I got smarter and faster, and I learned simple tactics
that improved my results in each race. I learned to stay with the pack at all
costs. I learned to be observant, and ride with the faster and smarter
riders. I learned how to conserve energy by using as few bursts as
possible. And I learned how far I could sprint before I "blew up," which
is when your muscles are so loaded with lactic acid they burn, and they
have no push left.

As I continued to race, I placed higher and higher in the field. I still
hadn't managed to put everything together that I needed to win, but I
began to think that sooner or later I would.

Finally, coming into the home stretch in one race, I was near the front
of the pack. Some of the riders began their sprint, but it was a bit too early
for me. I waited. When I was at the right spot, I stood up and pushed—

hard. My feet whirled, spinning the pedals around in what seemed like smaller and smaller circles. I caught the riders in front of me. Then I saw no more bikes.

You feel a kind of nervousness when you're being chased—excitement and fear feel the same. The fear snarls at you from behind, but the excitement buffers it away, at the same time driving you harder and harder. I pushed on, and the pedal circles got smaller.

The finish was approaching. I knew I had enough burst energy to make it there, but no farther. I still couldn't see anyone, but a rabbit knows he's being chased. My thighs burned. I pushed on. The burning erupted, searing from the inside out, and the pedal circles got no smaller. I crossed the finish line still pushing as hard as I could. The race was over, and no one was in front of me. I won.

But there's more to it than that. Consider Bill, a friend of mine who is a Cat III racer and who comes in last in nearly every race he participates in at this level. He often gets lapped during criteriums, or dropped from the pack, but he's out there week after week, rain or shine, always smiling and holding his head high. He does it because he loves to ride.

That's what bicycling is all about.

10

Maintaining Your Bike

Like a car, a well-maintained bike is safer, more efficient, and more enjoyable to ride. Routine maintenance isn't difficult or time-consuming, but unless you make it routine, it can seem more like a chore than a good idea.

I know you've heard it before, but I'm going to say it anyway: Use the right tool for the job. Buy and use metric tools if that's what fits your bike. They're not very expensive, and you'll be happier in the long run than if you improvise or try to adapt a near-fitting standard tool. Use open-end wrenches and box-end wrenches, not socket wrenches, to make adjustments on your bike. You can easily damage small nuts with the leverage you can apply with socket wrenches. An adjustable wrench should be used only in emergencies. Many adjustments can be made with hex keys on modern bikes.

BRAKES

Keep your brakes properly adjusted. The shoes should contact the rim simultaneously. Replace any frayed cables or rusted nuts and any worn brake shoes. Some bikes—usually racing and street models—have side-pull brakes. This means the cable runs to the side of one of the brakesets. A tool called a "third hand" greatly helps in adjusting side-pull brakes. This tool does exactly what its name implies—it acts as a hand to hold the brake shoes against the rim. It sure beats using a piece of string.

To adjust the side-pull brakes, position the third hand around the mounting nuts on the brake shoes. Loosen the ferrule through which the brake cable runs and pull the cable through. When it's tight, push it back

This is the side-pull brake. To remove the wheel, lift the lever on the left of the brake, as shown.

slightly, just to allow slack so the brake shoes don't contact the rim when the brake isn't applied. Carefully tighten the cable nut with a small, properly fitting wrench. Don't use a socket wrench. The nut can strip easily, but it must be snug enough so the cable doesn't slip through during hard braking.

Most cantilever brakes have a fine adjusting screw on the right cantilever arm (as you're facing the bike). Set the left arm as close to the rim as possible (but not so close that the rim hits the brake pad as it spins), then turn the adjusting screw until the right brake pad is the same distance from the rim as its partner.

Less expensive cantilever brakesets have no adjusting screw. Instead, you must remove the cable, as if you were removing the tire, and try to "uncoil" the cantilever arm's return spring by rotating each cantilever arm outward.

Adjusting a side-pull brake is easy with the aid of a "third-hand" tool.

The cantilever brake is more complex than the side-pull, but it provides a greater mechanical advantage, which is translated as more braking power for less effort.

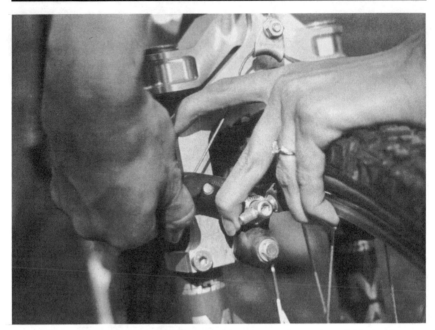

Slipping a mountain bike's tire through the cantilever brake requires you to remove the cable. Release tension from the cable by pushing in on the left cantilever arm; then unhook the cable.

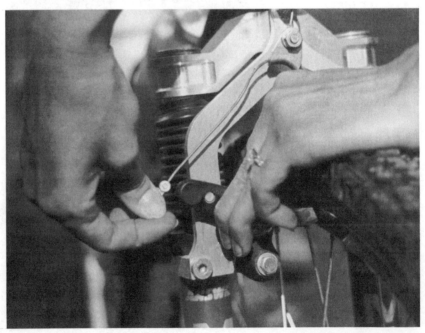

For coarse adjustment, remove the mounting screw that holds the cantilever arm to the fork and move the pin to the hole (there are usually three) that positions the shoe closest to the rim without touching it.

Expensive brakesets often have no adjusting screw, either. For all adjustments, loosen the mounting nut behind the cantilever arm, adjust the arm close to the rim (again, so the brake pad doesn't touch it), and tighten the nut.

HELMET

Make sure your helmet is in good shape. You should consider it as much a part of your bike as your pedals. Make sure it fits you well and hasn't been subjected to shocks. Any loss of integrity in the helmet, such as cracks, chips, frayed or broken straps, or a loose fit, should warrant replacement or the manufacturer's inspection of this important safety device (see Chapter 3).

CHAIN

Use a light lubricant such as WD-40 on your chain. An oil that's too heavy and thick will collect grit and dirt, which will wear your chain and

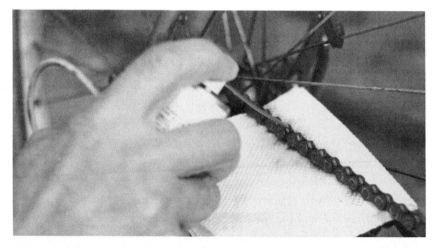

When lubricating the chain, hold a rag or absorbent paper towel under and behind the chain so oil won't get on the rim's braking surface.

sprockets faster. Special chain lubes are available, some containing Teflon or silicon, but I've never noticed any difference between those and WD-40 or similar products.

Wipe the rollers to remove excess grime before you oil the chain. Then, holding a rag or paper towel behind the chain, lightly coat the chain with oil, taking care not to get the spray on the rim, tire, or brake pad. (That's why you hold the rag behind the chain.) Now go for a ride. Like the way that feels? Remember it.

Spray your chain as needed, which is probably about every 200 miles. You'll spray more often if you've been riding in the rain or strictly in the city. If you've been riding on a trail, you may have to clean and lube the chain before each ride—dust and dirt, even on smooth trails, can quickly cake a chain. It takes only a few minutes to oil it; both you and the bike will feel better for it.

WHEELS

True wheels, wheels that spin without wobbling, are the key to a steady ride and essential for adjusting your brakes properly. If a wheel spins out of true, you must set the brake shoes farther away from the rim, and perhaps at uneven distances. Wheels can wobble from side to side and may also have a flat spot or "hop" in them. Either a wobble or a hop will give you a less smooth ride.

You can true a wheel yourself, but there's a knack to it. Wheel-truing can be frustrating, even for the pros. One large wobble can turn into three small ones. But with persistence and practice, you can true your own wheels.

You'll need a spoke wrench to fit the spoke nipples on your bike (spoke nipples come in different sizes; take your wheel—or bike—to your bike shop to make sure you get the right size). Avoid spoke wrenches that fit spokes of many sizes—they're of inferior quality and can quickly round the corners off the nipple, thus making the spokes very difficult to adjust. A truing stand will help greatly. This stand holds the wheel precisely between two adjustable guides.

To true the wheel, remove the tire and tube from the rim. (If you're checking only for wobble, just let all the air out of the tube.) Now set up the wheel in the truing stand. You must remember that every other spoke goes to the left side of the hub, and, of course, the others go to the right side. Since you never adjust just one spoke, you'll be turning

A truing stand and good spoke wrench will enable you to take the wobbles out and keep them out.

spokes in opposite directions, thus "pulling and pushing" the rim to make it straight.

Also remember that the nipple screws onto the spoke, but when you look at the nipple from the center of the wheel, it's as though you're looking at a screw upside-down. Therefore, a counterclockwise turn of the nipple will tighten the spoke, or make it "shorter," thus pulling the rim to the side of the hub to which the spoke goes.

In a nutshell, with the wheel in front of you, consider the chart on page 165.

It will take some getting used to (which is another good reason for turning the nipple very slightly), but once you're accustomed to it, making the rim go where you want will be second nature.

Check for roundness of the wheel first. Your truing stand makes this

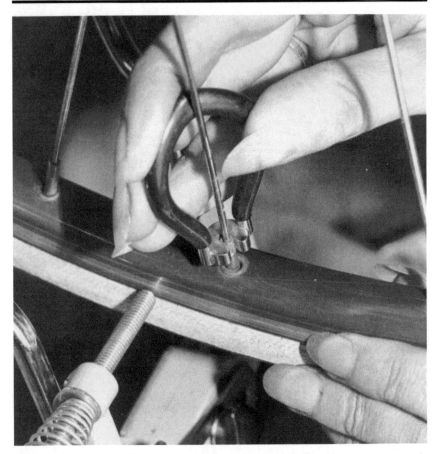

When truing a wheel, turn the spokes by very small fractions of an inch or you'll turn them too far. Here's how it's done.

easy. There's an adjustable plate on the front of the adjustable arm. Line that plate so that it just grazes the wheel. Spin the wheel easily. The gap between the wheel and the plate should remain constant throughout the revolution of the wheel. If it doesn't, align the high (or low) spot with the plate. Adjust the spokes a little at a time (1/16 of a turn, max). For a high spot, you must pull the rim back, so you'll want to "shorten" the spokes. Therefore, the spokes going to the right side of the hub will be turned counterclockwise; those going to the left side of the hub will be turned clockwise. The opposite will happen to "lengthen" the spokes to correct a low spot.

ART 10-8A

		If spoke goes to LEFT side of hub...	If spoke goes to RIGHT side of hub...
NIPPLE SPOKE	turn nipple COUNTER-CLOCKWISE...	to move rim LEFT. (spoke gets "shorter")	to move rim RIGHT. (spoke gets "shorter")
RIM	turn nipple CLOCKWISE...	to move rim RIGHT. (spoke gets "longer")	to move rim LEFT. (spoke gets "longer")

When the wheel has become a true circle again, check for a wobble (the wheel "jumps" to one side) by turning both knobs on the adjustable arm until they barely contact the rim. Spin the wheel. For a wheel that's badly out of true, you may have to back out the alignment screws so it will spin. If the wheel wobbles, correct the wobble by "shortening" or "lengthening" the spokes as you did above.

Quick-release wheels are a wonderful convenience for fixing flats and removing the wheel to load the bike onto a roof rack, but you must adjust the skewers properly—they must be tight enough to hold your wheel in the dropouts, but not so tight that you can't get the wheel off without fighting with it.

A skewer substitutes for a nut. Just as a nut can be too tight or too loose, so can a skewer. Open the skewer and fit the wheel into place. You should meet very light resistance just past the halfway point, moderate resistance at about the three-quarter point, and firm (but not excessive) resistance in the closed position. You should have to use the heel of your hand to close the lever completely, but you shouldn't have to lean into it or grunt to close the thing.

If your wheel's skewer is too loose or too tight, adjust the nut on the

This is a quick-release skewer removed from the wheel. Adjusting the black nut on the left end of the skewer will determine the maximum pressure you can apply to the fork to hold your wheel on.

opposite side of the quick-release lever and try again. You'll get the hang of it. Ask your bike mechanic if you're unsure about the proper setup.

Some quick-release mechanisms have a safety feature that prevents the wheel from falling out of the dropout if the skewer is too loose. This feature requires that the locking hub be unscrewed before removing the wheel. Properly adjusted quick-release mechanisms are safe, so don't panic if your bike isn't equipped with this safety feature. Its use is to convert quick-release wheels to slow-release wheels.

TIRES

Keep your tires inflated to the proper air pressure, which you can find on the tire's sidewall. Tires leak air when they're just sitting, as well as when they're in use. Very narrow tires (700C×20, 700C×23, 27"×1", etc.) have a low profile, so the tubes can easily be pinched between the rim and tire if the air pressure is too low. This pinching is called a "snakebite" because the two holes in the tube make it look like it's been bitten by a snake. Don't use a gas-station pump to fill your tires with

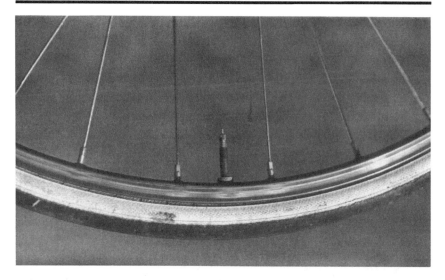

This is a Presta valve, one of two types available on bike tubes. The Presta has been more common in Europe than in this country but is now available on many bikes in the U.S. You'll always see it on high-performance bike tubes.

This is a Schrader valve. It's the type used on car tires and on many mountain bikes.

air. They pump much too fast and can easily blow out a bicycle tire with excessive pressure.

Mountain-bike tires are more liberal with the air pressure they can use. The sidewall prints the maximum pressure, but you may want to reduce the pressure considerably for more traction and comfort on the trail. Be careful, though—you can damage your rim if the tire is too soft to provide protection from rocks.

Higher air pressure lets the tire find the bottom of soft terrain, while the lower air pressure lets the tire ride on top, as a snowshoe more evenly distributes your body weight on top of snow. Minimum pressure depends on the tire. Lower pressure gives a softer, more cushioned ride and provides better traction, but makes the bike harder to pedal. Know your tires and how they respond to your body weight and riding style. If you're riding only on the road, the maximum pressure will be fine.

Although repairing flat tires isn't a maintenance procedure, it's probably the most common task you'll have to perform next to oiling your chain. To patch a small puncture, locate the leak (while the tube is still in the tire) by partially inflating the tire and slowly spinning the wheel, listening carefully for escaping air.

When you hear the air escaping, press on the tire with your fingertip until the rushing sound stops. (Sometimes, when traffic is heavy, it's difficult to hear the air escaping. Try bringing your lips or cheek close to the tire so you can feel the stream of air.) That's the puncture. Mark it, and make sure there are no other punctures. Can you hear any more air escaping when you cover the hole with your fingertip? Or does the tire stop getting flatter?

When you're sure you've found all the leaks (usually there's only one leak, although snakebites will give you two), completely deflate the tire. Remove the puncturing object if it's still in the tire.

If you can't find the leak, completely remove the tube from the rim, partially inflate it, and immerse it in a bucket of water. The puncture is at the origin of the stream of bubbles. Now carefully feel inside the tire for the offending object. Be careful—it may be sharp, like glass or a tack. Remove the object and inspect the puncture.

Remove the tire from the rim by slipping a nylon tire lever under the tire bead (the hard "cords"—there's one below each tire's sidewall—that hook into the rim so the tire doesn't fall off) two inches to the left of the puncture and pry the tire from the rim. Hook the lever onto a spoke.

To remove a tire from the rim, slip a nylon tire lever under the tire bead two inches to the left of the puncture. Repeat two inches to the right of the puncture with another tire lever, pry the tire from the rim, and pull a portion of the tube from beneath the tire.

(Continued)

Follow instructions in the text (or in your patch kit) and cover the puncture with a patch. Then replace the tube in the tire and the tire onto the rim.

Repeat this two inches to the right of the puncture with a second lever. Slide the first lever a few more inches away from the puncture to "unhook" more of the tire; then hook the lever on a nearby spoke. Repeat for the second lever. Pull the tube—only as much as you need to repair the leak—from beneath the tire.

Cover the puncture with a patch for bike tubes. The patch kit, which is available from your bike shop, includes enough patches and rubber cement for at least an entire season. But buy a new kit at the beginning of each riding season—the rubber cement dries up.

In your patch kit you'll find sandpaper or a scraper, rubber cement, and patches. Roughen the tube around the puncture with the sandpaper or scraper. Then squeeze about a 3/8-inch dot of rubber cement centered on the puncture, and spread it with your finger so that it covers an area slightly larger than the diameter of the patch. (The patch won't stick to the tube, only to the rubber cement.) When the rubber cement is completely dry (about three to five minutes), peel the backing from the patch and center it over the puncture.

If the tire was sliced rather than punctured, or if the hole in the tire is otherwise so large that the tube will bulge through it when completely inflated, you must put a tire boot (a one- to two-inch section cut from an old tire) between the hole in the tire and the patch on the tube. Replace the tube in the tire and replace the tire onto the rim. You're always advised not to use the tire levers to pry the tire back onto the tube, but some tire beads are so stiff that I've had to. No ill effects resulted, but don't use the levers if it isn't necessary; you can bend the bead. Inflate the tire to half the recommended pressure and inspect the rim and tire to make sure the tube isn't bulging from between the tire and rim. Then inflate the tire to full pressure.

Maintaining a bicycle is like maintaining a car—you can change the oil yourself, but not everyone has the ability, time, desire, or tools to replace a blown head gasket. Routine maintenance of any moving part is a good idea, but some procedures are lengthy and complex. Consult a bicycle repair book or your bike shop for details and the tools you'll need for jobs such as overhauling the bottom bracket (the assembly to which the pedal crank is mounted) and adjusting the headset (the assembly which permits steering). If you have no desire to do the job yourself, most reputable bike shops employ excellent mechanics.

11

A Brief History of Bicycling

O liver Wendell Holmes (the elder), who was famous for his acute and witty observations of American life, commented in 1882 on the growing practicality of cycling as well as the unprecedented enthusiasm of cyclists, remarking that "wheels rush in where horses fear to tread."

An early advocate of exercise and fitness, Holmes loved to row a wherry, a swift, one-man racing boat ancestral to the racing scull. In 1857, in one of his essays in *The Autocrat of the Breakfast-Table,* he described his sport as "the nearest approach to flying that man has ever made and perhaps ever will make." By 1882, when a new edition of the book was published, he felt compelled to revise that statement in a long, historically intriguing footnote:

> Since the days when this was written the bicycle has appeared as a rival of the wherry. I have witnessed three appearances of the pedal locomotive. The first was when I was a boy....Some of the Harvard College students who boarded in my neighborhood had these machines, then called velocipedes, on which they used to waddle along like so many ducks, their feet pushing against the ground, looking like they were perched on portable treadmills. They soon learned that legs were made before velocipedes. Our grown-up young people may remember the second advent of the contrivance, now become a treadle-locomotive. There were "rinks" where this form of roller-skating had a brief run, and then legs again asserted their prior claim and greater convenience. At the Continental Exhibition in Philadelphia, in 1876, I first saw the modern [pedal-powered and easily steerable] bicycles, some of them, at least, from Coventry, England. Since that time [only six years] the bicycle glides in and out everywhere, noiseless as a serpent....The boat flies like a

This early 19th century print shows velocipedes, also known as hobby-horses, which had no pedals. The rider propelled the simple machine by thrusting one foot and then the other against the ground, as if skating. "They used to waddle along like so many ducks," wrote Oliver Wendell Holmes.

sea-bird with its long, narrow, outstretched pinions; the bicycle rider, like feathered Mercury, with his wings on his feet....

LEONARDO'S DREAM

The bicycle as we know it—or even as our great-great grandfathers knew it—has a very short history, yet the concept of cycling, the dream of this strange manner of locomotion, may well be many centuries old. In medieval iconography, the image of cherubim and seraphim riding on a wheel was not uncommon. Until 1966, historians of technology and of sport pretty well agreed that the first primitive bicycles appeared in the eighteenth century and the first pedaled versions in the nineteenth. But then the monks of Grottoferrata, near Rome, working on government-sponsored restorations of some of Leonardo da Vinci's manuscripts, discovered sketches made by his pupils in the 1490s. Among them were pornographic drawings, a caricature of a pupil, and a crude sketch of a two-wheeled, pedaled, chain-driven bicycle.

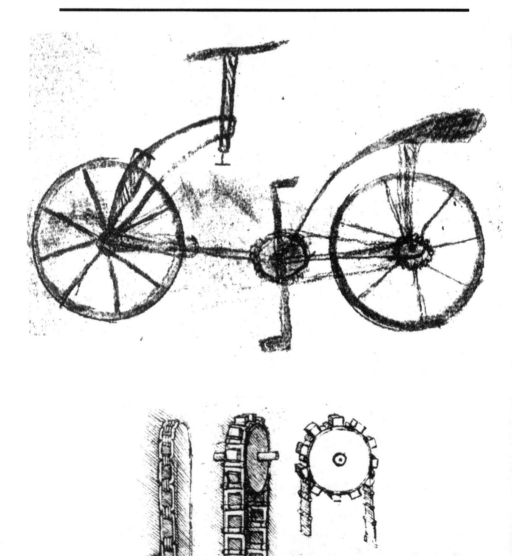

One of Leonardo de Vinci's pupils drew this rough sketch of a bicycle, circa 1490, presumably from a drawing or model made by Leonardo himself. Its pedals, chain drive, and overall plan are astonishing, for three and a half centuries were to pass before such a bicycle was reinvented and actually built. Leonardo's own drawings of a chain drive are also shown. The square teeth on the chainwheel would have prevented movement, but he later corrected that error with rounded teeth.

The machine would have been difficult if not impossible to ride, for the seat is too far to the rear and the one-piece frame seems to bracket the front wheel and prevent steering. All the same, it is a bicycle. Definitely not drawn by da Vinci himself, it presumably was copied from one of his drawings or models or based on his instructions. Evidently Leonardo, the genius who drew plans for a submarine, an aircraft, and a wheel-lock firearm among other inventions, invented the bicycle as well. If so, his original drawing or model was lost and his idea forgotten until independently reinvented centuries later.

Children's hobbyhorses had been popular since the Middle Ages and were the inspiration for the first known bicycle—without pedals or other mechanical drive—which appeared in 1791. That was the year an eccentric young Parisian aristocrat, the Comte de Sivrac, demonstrated a wheeled wooden horse in the gardens of the Palais Royal. It had a small saddle, but no pedals or steering mechanism. The rider straddled the contrivance and propelled it by thrusting one foot and then the other along the ground, pushing hard to gain speed—waddling like a duck, as Holmes later described the procedure. Having gained some momentum, a rider could lift his feet and glide for short distances, but without any foot rests this was awkward. To turn, the rider had to put one or both feet on the ground while lifting or shoving the hobbyhorse head to one side or the other.

Despite these major difficulties, the *célerifère*, as the Comte called it (or celeripede, as the English called it) attained quick popularity. Taken from the Latin *celeritas*, the name literally meant "speedster." Two years after its appearance and for unknown reasons, it was renamed the vélocifère— which meant the same thing—and a club of young men calling themselves the Vélocipèdes organized and conducted races on the Champs Elysées, history's first recorded bicycle races.

Across the channel, England's young men called the machine itself a velocipede, but for decades it was also called the hobbyhorse or dandy-horse—apparently an allusion to the riders, many of whom were foppishly dressed bachelors showing off for laughing and cheering audiences of young women. Inevitably, many of the young women demanded their turn on the velocipedes, either waddling solo or riding behind a male waddler, and longer-beamed velocipedes were introduced to accommodate two waddlers.

The first great mechanical improvement came in Mannheim, Germany, in 1817, when Karl, Baron von Drais de Sauerbrun, devised a steerable front wheel by passing a front fork through a simple socket. Known as the Draisienne, his version had a cushioned saddle (lacking on some earlier models) and a rest for the rider's arms, which made the footwork easier and facilitated steering. The Baron, a superintendent of forests for the Duke of Baden, used his Draisienne to ride the forest paths, thus becoming the world's first known mountain biker.

His machine also carried the first known accessory, a simple distance gauge, or odometer, fitted to the rear wheel in 1825. Even without pedals, the bicycle had already become more than an amusing novelty. Not only did the Baron use one to speed his rounds of inspection, but for a short period rural French mail carriers used them in place of horses or foot travel. All the same, healthful exercise and diversion remained the chief roles of the bicycles—too often accompanied by thrill-seeking reckless riding that aroused public indignation and ridicule in the press. The poet John Keats, certain that bicycles would soon be forgotten, called them "the 'nothing' of the day."

THE AGE OF
THE VELOCIPEDES

Roads in the early nineteenth century were so poor that much cycling was done on sidewalks and footpaths, occasionally leading to collisions with pedestrians and often resulting in spills. Velocipedes inspired such outrage in Milan that in 1818 they were banned from that city. For a decade or so, however, their popularity spread in spite of all objections, although it dwindled in England. Johann Wolfgang von Goethe watched the students of Jena riding their "running machines" (also known as quick walkers and pedestrian curricles) on an outdoor gymnastics mall, and in the Netherlands the mayor of Haarlem owned one.

By the spring of 1819, velocipedes were being manufactured in Massachusetts for both sale and rent. They were "hired out" for 25 cents an hour. Harvard students delighted in riding on moonlit nights, and a brief velocipeding craze seized the Eastern Seaboard. After Dennis Johnson, a London designer, manufacturer, and riding-school operator, arrived in New York in 1819, rinks, bicycle ways, and riding schools were established there and in other eastern cities.

The American press, like its English counterpart, was critical. On July 9,

1819, the *Federal Republican and Baltimore Telegraph* advised its readers that "A curious two-wheeled vehicle called the velocipede has been invented, which is propelled by Jack-asses instead of horses." New York City followed Milan's example and prohibited bicycle riding for some years.

TREADLE POWER, PEDAL POWER

During these same years, a succession of mechanical improvements appeared. Johnson's wood and iron velocipedes were somewhat better built than the Draisiennes, and in 1821 Lewis Gompertz of Surry, England, introduced a kind of hand treadle to supplement leg power. He used a steering column to which was attached a toothed quadrant that engaged a pinion on the front wheel hub. The rider pulled backward on a handlebar atop the column to move the front wheel forward. Within the next two decades, a number of experimental tricycles and quadricycles appeared, with various hand and foot cranks for locomotion. And in 1839, a Scottish blacksmith named Kirkpatrick Macmillan built a two-wheeler with axle bearings and a pedaled foot-treadle.

Despite these attempts at improvement, interest in velocipedes waned. Said to produce hernias faster than they produced muscles, they were, after all, heavy, cumbersome, fatiguing, brakeless, and seldom capable of greater speed than perhaps fifteen miles an hour. With more speed than that, they would have been uncontrollable. In about 1860 Macmillan's machine did acquire a rear-wheel brake, but there is a legend, possibly true, that the inventor himself was once fined five shillings when one of his contraptions injured a child.

Many great inventions are so simple, so obvious, as to make us marvel that no one had thought of them sooner. Bicycle pedals are a monumental case in point. In 1861, a Parisian hatter ordered his hobbyhorse repaired at the shop of Pierre Michaux, a builder of perambulators and tricycles. After a disheartening road test, Michaux and his two sons discussed possible ways to improve the slow, awkward machine, and Michaux père suggested that it might be accomplished by fitting a cranked axle to the front hub, "like the crank handle of a grindstone, so that it could be turned by the feet of the rider."

His son Ernest carried out the suggestion, converting the hobbyhorse into a pedal-power prototype. At Bar-le-Duc a national monument com-

This is the Gompertz velocipede of 1821. By leaning against the chest rest and pulling rearward on the handlebar, the rider made the front wheel turn, pulling the velocipede forward.

Velocipedes gained considerable maneuverability and speed after steerable handlebars were added and Pierre Michaux invented a pedal system. This is an American 1869 "sprung" velocipede, an attempt to reduce jolts and vibrations.

memorates their achievement as *"inventeurs et propagateurs du vélocipède à pédale."*

The *vélocipède à pédale* was not without drawbacks. By 1865, Michaux was producing 400 bicycles a year, but also dealing with complaints that the pedals on the front wheel caused a steering problem—the difficulty of turning the wheel to one side or the other while pedaling. Doing so brought the iron rim into contact with the rider's leg, which caused chafing (and probably occasional bruising) as well as trouser damage. A riding manual advised that a cycling pupil "may fairly add the value of six pairs of trousers to his outlay." Furthermore, the ride on rough roads remained heavy and jarring. On muddy dirt or wet pavement, the bicycle slipped, hopped, and skidded.

Improvements accelerated faster than the machines themselves. By 1869, rubber tires (solid at first) appeared on vehicles ranging from bicycles to buggies, relatively light wire bicycle spokes were introduced, and Jules Suriray patented and produced ball bearings for the wheel hubs. By then, in fact, steel racing bicycles had been introduced. Even a handlebar-mounted brake, connected to the rear rim, had made its appearance. Tubular frames, spring-mounted front wheels, and spring-mounted saddles quickly followed. And in 1871, wonder of wonders, a device for tensioning the spokes actually removed some of the wobbles.

THE HIGH-WHEELED BONESHAKERS

The high bicycle, high-wheeler, "ordinary," or "penny-farthing," as it was often called, evolved gradually during the 1860s and '70s. No one knows who first called it a "boneshaker," but that may have been the most common as well as the most descriptive nickname of all. On the Michaux velocipede, the front wheel had been slightly larger than the rear. Other makers followed suit, and the front wheel just kept on growing to achieve the highest possible ratio between one pedal revolution and one wheel revolution.

At its height of popularity its literal height ranged from shoulder-level to forehead level, making mounting and starting a challenge to strength, coordination, and balance. The trailing wheel might be only a foot or two high and sometimes as low as six inches! There ensued experiments in techniques of mounting, none without problems. What looked easiest was to prop the monstrous bicycle against an upright support and climb

This is the Ariel, one of the most popular high-wheelers—or "boneshakers"—of the 1870s. All metal but lighter than most, it was the first to have solid rubber tires and spokes that could be tightened.

aboard with the aid of a step-stool or anything else that would let you get a leg up. But to take off from a standing start required considerable power as well as balance. You were more likely to topple than wobble.

Most true high-wheelers were therefore equipped with a little foot-rest over the small rear wheel or slightly higher on the frame. You grasped the handlebar and stepped back behind the bike, stretching and learning to maintain your hold. Then you trotted a step or two, placed one foot on the rest, shoved mightily with the other foot to overcome inertia, and leaped aboard as you gained momentum. Despite these physical demands, high-wheelers (sometimes smaller or modified versions of the full-size models) became popular among young women as well as men. At Bordeaux in 1868, women racers were cheered by an enthusiastic road-side audience.

Cycling clubs soon attained large memberships in Britain, the United States, and on the Continent. Among the most famous high-wheel cycling meets was an annual affair initiated in 1876 at Hampton Court Palace near London. Six years later the meet drew 2,177 cyclists who rode in an opening-ceremony procession, club after club, six miles long.

Thomas Humber was a famous English maker of high-wheelers. The many variations included tandems like this 1885 Humber model.

The high-wheeler inspired some bizarre variations, including a tricycle built for two and bicycles employing a high *rear* wheel, with the rider mounted over the rear rim and pedals or a treadle flanking the rear hub. Still, by far the most common was the standard "ordinary" or "penny-farthing" (a reference to the difference in front and rear wheel size).

Accidents were frequent and could be serious. Careening downhill at 30 miles an hour, an agile rider might drape his legs over the handlebar, not only to keep his feet away from the spinning pedals but also to increase the chance that with luck he would be thrown clear of the wheel in the event of a "header." Many a boneshaker weighed over 50 pounds. Becoming entangled with a 50-pound whir of metal hurtling into an obstacle or the ground was a decidedly dangerous prospect. All the same, road and track races and organized rallies such as 50-mile rides were common—and occasionally stopped by the police.

THE CHAIN-DRIVEN
SAFETY BICYCLE

Although Kirkpatrick Macmillan had experimented with and demonstrated rear drive, for several decades the novel idea failed to inspire improved designs or capture a market. Manufacturers of boneshakers tried various modifications of their basic designs, such as a somewhat reduced front wheel, braking devices, and gearing to allow the front wheel to revolve faster than the pedals (or conversely, from the user's standpoint, to allow the pedals to revolve more slowly). Such models were occasionally labeled safety bicycles, but they were not sufficiently safe to establish the common use of that term except perhaps in the press and advertisements.

The first true safety bicycles, as they came to be known for many years, were low-slung machines with wheels of nearly equal diameter (the front or rear wheel was only slightly enlarged), employing chain drive from the pedals to the rear wheel.

The safety bicycles that began to appear more or less commonly on the roads in the mid-1880s were, in other words, the first modern bikes. Probably the earliest such design, evidently unpatented and never built, was by F. W. Shearing and appeared in the *English Mechanic* in 1869. About seven years later, George Shergold of Gloucester, England, built a roughly similar one which survives in the London Science Museum. At around the same time, a builder in Marseilles produced one with the chain drive connected to the front wheel, which must have been harder to pedal and failed to attract much interest.

Another English designer, H. J. Lawson, patented a "Bicyclette" in 1879, and it was exhibited at a bike show the following year by the Tangent Bicycle Company. Regarded as the first true, rear-drive safety bicycle to make an impact on builders or customers, the Lawson Bicyclette had a 40-inch front wheel, a 24-inch rear wheel, a headlight lantern, and a needlessly complex indirect steering mechanism with coupling rods extending from a handle to the front fork.

Moderately popular at best, this bicycle exerted far more influence on designers than on the public. It was an ugly little machine, more commonly known as the Crocodile than Bicyclette, and such famous racing champions of the time as Lacy Hillier remained loudly loyal to their high-wheel "ordinaries." But manufacturers—as eccentric or visionary, depending on one's point of view, as the American, French, German, and British aircraft designers a generation later—slowly, surely, stubbornly evolved improvements based on the Lawson-type safety bicycle.

In 1884, several British makers introduced low, rear-drive bicycles, and in 1885, the Rover, designed by John Kemp Starley and built by the British firm of Starley & Sutton, "set the fashion to the world" just as its

The Lawson 1879 Bicyclette was the first true, rear-drive safety bicycle to exert an influence on future bicycle construction. It was derisively called the Crocodile, but its chain system and reduced difference in front and rear wheel size had advantages quickly recognized by designers.

manufacturer claimed. Weighing 37 pounds, it had a front wheel only slightly larger than the rear and a rearward-curved handlebar that provided direct steering.

It might have been overlooked as merely another "dwarf" novelty bike had the manufacturer not devised a brilliant publicity stunt: the Rover Road Race of September, 1885, for Rover riders only, over a 100-mile course. The faster competitors on those Rovers eclipsed the speeds recorded for the swiftest high-wheelers in comparable previous races. The winner was an experienced racing champion, George Smith, who broke the world record by crossing the finish line after 7 hours, 5 minutes, and 16 seconds. If an average speed of just over 14 miles an hour seems amusingly unimpressive by today's standards, it should be remembered that this was an endurance race over hilly, often rough-surfaced roads on single-gear bicycles. The manufacturer was now able to advertise the Rover not only as a safety bicycle but also as a speed model.

The Rover set the fashion in other ways, too. It had adjustable handlebar and seat positions, and a changeable chainwheel and rear sprocket so that gearing could be altered. A second and third model, each slightly improved, came in quick succession, and the third had—at last—wheels of equal size and a "diamond frame," the pattern on which makers would base their future designs. The Rover earned such international acclaim that its name came to stand for its general type of design, and in a manner of speaking still does in some countries. The Polish word for bicycle is *rower*—pronounced "Rover."

Acceptance, however, was not at first universal. The early safeties, solid-tired of course, were said to vibrate even more than the high-wheeled bone-shakers. Moreover, the pedals of a low-wheeled bike were so low that mud splashed the rider's feet and legs, and it was claimed that the chain drive wasted power in transferring it. On the other hand, as models improved, riders rejoiced that the "free steering" (unaffected by pedaling, with the front wheel distanced from the cyclist's legs) was effortless rather than strain-inducing; the long wheelbase reduced the frequency and severity of side-slips while also allowing for luggage bags and racks over one or both wheels;

This is the 1885 Rover safety bicycle, which still retained the high-wheeler foot rest at the back of the frame so the rider could shove off from the rear. This was no longer really necessary, since a person of average height could straddle it. The Rover proved to be much speedier than previous designs, and it became world famous.

By the late 1880s, bicycles with front and rear wheels of more or less equal size were becoming common. This safety bicycle is an 1888 Raleigh. Within a few years, Raleighs with wheels of equal size were being used by many of the great racing champions.

hill climbing was much easier; and, as one author has vividly noted, such a bicycle "took the terror out of a fast downhill run."

DUNLOP'S SAUSAGE-TIRES

Some of the faster safety bicycles, such as the 1887 Whippet, reduced the severity of hard-ride bumpiness by means of sprung frame suspension and a sprung saddle, and by 1888 manufacturers were turning out far more low bicycles than high ones.

That was the year when John Boyd Dunlop, a Scottish veterinary surgeon working in Belfast, tinkered with his young son's tricycle in an effort to improve its riding characteristics. Rubber tires had been in common use for years by then, but they were solid rubber strips that cushioned wheel bounce and vibration only in minor degree. Although a rubber strip was considerably better than a naked steel rim or a strip of steel around a wood-

John Sloan, who gained fame in the world of fine art as well as advertising, painted this poster for Apollo Bicycles in the late 1890s. The ladies' model shown has typical rearward-raked handlebars and, quite obviously, air-filled tires.

en wheel, far too much kinetic energy was still transferred to machine and rider for comfort and steady control. Perceiving that the wheels rather than the rider needed greater cushioning, Dunlop experimented by fitting air-filled tires to the tricycle.

Merely to say the idea worked is about like saying wheels improved mobility. The Pneumatic Tyre Company was founded, the name Dunlop became as closely associated with inflatable tires as the name Rover with early modern bicycles, and such tires literally revolutionized the concept of bicycling throughout the world. There were, of course, flat tires and blow-outs—far more than with today's tires, enormously improved through high technology and modern materials—and Dunlop's invention was popularly known by such epithets as bladder-wheel, windbag, pudding-tire, and sausage-tire. However, if these nicknames were at first used derisively, they were soon used affectionately.

(Cyclists are entitled to note with smug amusement that their forebears were quicker to accept inflatable tires than early motorists would be. When automobiles finally began to appear on the roads, most had solid tires, evidently because of worry that air-filled rubber would not support great weight.)

Even before the advent of the pneumatic tire, police and mail carriers in many parts of the world were getting about on bicycles, and in 1886 the Cyclists' Touring Club in England boasted more than 20,000 members. The French army had been audacious enough to put high-wheelers into limited use, but the more compact safety bicycles proved to be far more practical, especially with the new tires. Bicycles came into more common use by military couriers and signal corpsmen, and were now enormously more efficient not only for racing and park riding but for touring and even for going to business or school over cobblestoned city streets. Then, as more cities began to pave their streets smoothly, cycling attracted still greater numbers of enthusiasts. Coin-operated air pumps were installed along roadsides in the United States and several other countries. (A dime was generally the price of a fill-up in this country.)

PROTECTION FOR AND FROM CYCLISTS

During that first, largely unregulated peak of cycling mania, grave concern arose for the safety of cyclists and their potential victims, and many nations enacted the first traffic laws pertaining to bicycles. In England, for example, an 1888 Act of Parliament granted the bicycle status as a type of "carriage" entitled to road space—provided the rider kept a bell ringing continuously while in motion. Bells and horns, as ineffectual then as now, began to sound on the roads and paths of the United States, England, Europe, and Asia.

Horses shied, dogs barked and snapped at wheels and heels, blacksmiths protested (fearing the demise of horseshoeing), and pedestrians shook their fists. Bicycle accessories soon included squeeze bottles of repellent to ward off dogs, and in France and Belgium handlebar pistols were manufactured in pairs, one for each side. The business end of such a pistol was attached to or inserted into the hollow (cut off) end of the handlebar, and the pistol grip became the handlebar grip. A vigorous pull would detach the gun for instant use. That such extreme and bizarre measures never attained great popularity may be a credit to the common sense of cyclists. All the same, in the United States some riders carried small, cheap pocket pistols known by sensational brand names like Tramp's Terror and Bulldog. Whether their chief purpose was really protection from aggressive animals and highwaymen or a show of force against indignant sharers of the roads is open to speculation.

During the last two decades of the nineteenth century, overstuffed Victorians began to heed the advice of physicians and amateur fitness advocates who urged them to get outdoors, breathe deeply of the fresh air, improve their spiritual health through communion with nature, and exercise regularly by cycling, hiking, canoeing, and camping. Americans seemed to be trying to out-exercise the English.

Conspicuous consumption may have had something to do with it. Influential people publicized the trend. John D. Rockefeller—who was not, himself, an ardent cyclist—presented bicycles to a number of friends whose health concerned him. Presidents William McKinley of the United States and Félix Faure of France, both wishing to show themselves off as men of the people, rode plain middle-class bikes, while nouveau riche celebrities like Diamond Jim Brady leaned toward lavish, custom-built ostentation.

Brady had ten gold-plated presentation bikes built. As he was infatuated with the singer-actress Lillian Russell, he gave her one with her monogram engraved on each gold part, mother-of-pearl handlebar grips, a huge amethyst centered on the handlebar, and gem-encrusted spokes. She was not foolish enough to ride it much, but it went on tour with her in a lined leather case.

Plain folk, though they rode plain bikes, craved speed and mobility, and since city streets were in general smoother than country roads, cyclists swarmed through cities. One day in 1897, an estimated 25,000 riders used a single New York City road. Accidents increased, fights

Here's an 1896 advertising poster by Will Bradley (one of the era's most popular cycling illustrators) for a racing tournament organized and conducted by the Springfield Bicycle Club. Springfield Diamond Tournaments—named for the prizes, which were diamonds!—were among the most prestigious of American meets. The handlebars shown drop barely below the horizontal plane, but severely dropped handlebars were coming into vogue, and Washington, D.C., prohibited them to discourage speeding.

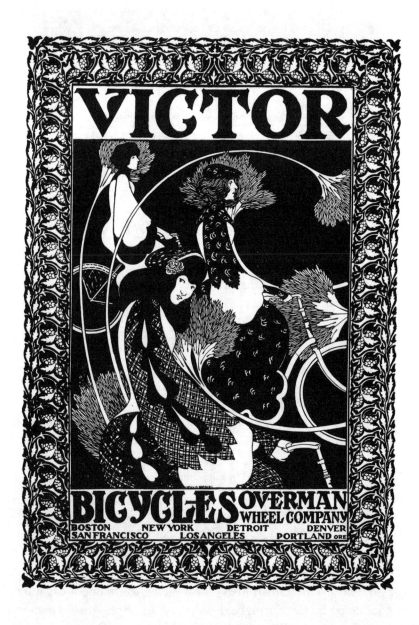

This is an 1896 gem of *art nouveau,* painted by Will Bradley for the Overman Wheel Company's Victor Bicycles. The bicycle industry made a strong appeal to women through an emphasis on fashion and elegance.

erupted between "wheelmen" and draymen, and as racing-style bikes with dropped handlebars came into vogue, cities like Washington, D.C., tried to control speeders by legislating that dropped handlebars could dip no lower than four inches below saddle level.

HOW BICYCLES CHANGED OUR CULTURE

Cycle paths were built, the dime-operated air pumps sprouted, and manufacturers had difficulty deciding whether frivolity was beneficial to sales. They recommended black bicycles for widows in mourning, while a purveyor of accessories advertised a magnet, suspended ahead of the front wheel, to pick up nails and prevent punctures.

Annie Oakley fired her rifle at moving targets while riding a bicycle instead of a horse in Buffalo Bill's Wild West Show; New York City provided bikes for more than 100 street-cleaning inspectors; and the Salvation Army established a bicycle corps in New York and Chicago. Cycling Salvationists also visited mining camps in the West. As cycling clubs, magazines, and books proliferated, the influence of the clubs, staunchly supported by both the cycling and general press, led to road building, paving, maintenance, and improvement programs that began at about the turn of the century and continued intermittently through its seventh decade.

Over 400 cycling poems (mostly humorous) were written during the 1880s and '90s; many were set to music, and scores of cycling songs were composed. The most famous was "Daisy Bell," or "A Bicycle Built for Two," by an English cyclist who was visiting New York. Sadly, his name cannot be recorded with any certainty. He used the pen name Harry Dacre, but his real name is thought to have been Frank Dean or Henry Decker. The song became a sensational hit after Jenny Lindsay sang it at the Atlantic Gardens on New York's Bowery in 1894:

> Daisy, Daisy,
> Give me your answer, do,
> I'm half crazy
> All for the love of you.
> It won't be a stylish marriage,
> I can't afford a carriage,
> But you'll look sweet on the seat
> Of a bicycle built for two.

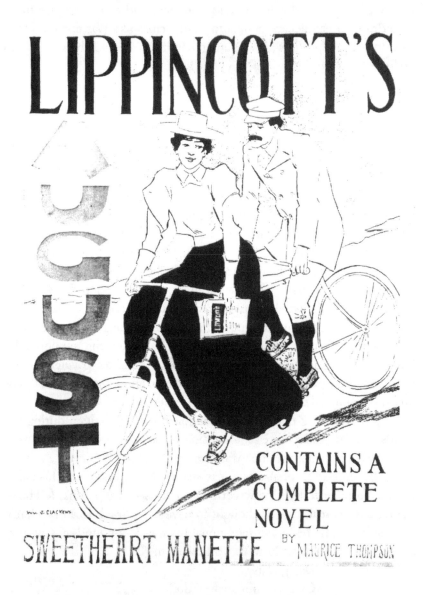

An 1894 advertisement—not for bicycles but for *Lippincott's* magazine—exploited the great popularity of tandem bikes.

Bicycles made fashion statements and were condemned as demonic by preachers. Business owners (other than haberdashers and bicycle shops) grumbled that money went for bikes and biking apparel instead of watches, snuff boxes, or houses. Barber shops and saloons lost customers who were in training. An accomplished rider named Margaret Gardner, who became the first woman to finish the Sag Harbor-to-Brooklyn run, in 1894, created an uproar with the comfortable bloomer costume she designed and wore. Her "immodest" outfit established an international fashion for about a generation, probably in part because bloomers, like men's knee-length "knickerbockers" of the time and the shortened skirts that later gained acceptance, seldom got caught in a chain sprocket.

Although the last decade of the nineteenth century was marked by general economic depression in the United States, it was the Gay Nineties for cyclists and the bicycle industry. In 1896 about 250 factories built well over a million bicycles, and some 600 makers of accessories employed an estimated 60,000 people.

In England and much of Europe, the long-established popularity of cycling swelled into a controversial craze, but opposition quickly succumbed to the inevitable. The famous novelist H. G. Wells and his wife toured the English countryside on separate bikes and on a bicycle built for two. Three early Wells novels—*History of Mr. Polly, Kipps,* and *The Wheels of Chance*—featured cycling.

In *The Wheels of Chance* (1896), which is regarded as a cycling classic, the plot, one might say, turns on bicycle wheels. A girl elopes on a bicycle, and a wonderful chase involves an antiquated tricycle (with two big wheels in front), a tandem tricycle, and a highly geared tandem bicycle. The hero, Hoopdriver, is a draper's assistant (as the author himself had been). On his annual vacation, Hoopdriver follows a route once taken by Wells as he sets out on a ten-day tour of England's South Coast, riding an old bicycle but dressed in a new brown cycling suit. The description of his experience evokes the kind of adventure riders still seek and find:

> Here was quiet and greenery, and one mucked about as the desire took one....Once he almost ran over something wonderful, a little, low red beast with a yellowish tail, that went rushing across the road before him. It was the first weasel he had ever seen in his cockney life. There were miles of this, scores of miles before him....

HUMBER & C° L^{TD}
32. HOLBORN VIADUCT. LONDON. E.C.

Like most bicycle posters showing both men and women, this advertisement for Humber bicycles showed the woman leading—in this case beckoning to her slower male companions to catch up. It also showed the bicycle's emancipating influence on women's attire in the 1890s. Bloomers scandalized Victorian notions of feminine modesty, but a well-known cyclist, Margaret Gardner, popularized them and set a new fashion.

Among the famous cycling enthusiasts at the turn of the century was the English novelist H. G. Wells, who not only rode bicycles but wrote about them. This illustration is from his 1896 novel, *The Wheels of Chance*, which has been called a cycling classic.

WHAT'S NEW AND WHAT ISN'T

Everything about today's bicycles makes those ridden by Wells and Hoopdriver seem primitive, and yet most of the features—excluding featherlight, ultrastrong materials, safety helmets, and accessories such as mountain-bike shock absorbers and handlebar computers—were in place by the turn of the century or shortly thereafter. Almost incredible improvements have blessed our ride, but they have chiefly been just that—improvements rather than completely new inventions.

Tandem bicycles were common in the nineteenth century, and both civilians and military forces experimented with two-piece and folding bikes during the last quarter of that century. Great Britain equipped a few troops with folding bikes made by BSA (Birmingham Small Arms) during the Boer War, and then or shortly afterward the Pope Manufacturing Company—a major pioneer of the American bicycle industry—built a combat bike mounting a Colt machine gun for the United States Army. The truth soon became self-evident, however, that bicycles are better suited to peaceful activities and courier service than to the battlefield.

There seems to be a fairly common misperception that adjustable spokes, hand-operated brakes, and shiftable multiple gears are relatively recent inventions. Even a few of the old boneshakers had adjustable spokes, and some had hand brakes (which became vastly safer and more effective when the front wheel shrank). Good-quality safety bicycles sometimes had more than one gear and offered the buyer a choice of hand-operated rim brakes or a coaster (pedal) brake.

The 1901 Dursley-Pedersen Gentleman's Model Royal, for example, was offered with a choice of braking systems in a single-gear version, while there were rim brakes, front and rear, on a three-speed version. Even with the three-speed shiftable gear and optional features, it was reasonably priced. Depending on size and features, it could weigh as little as 23 pounds, and it even had a frame-clipped tire pump.

DR. WHITE'S PRESCRIPTION

During the 1920s and 1930s, velodrome and road racing continued to be popular, especially in Europe, and bicycle camping was popular in the United States and England, yet most people regarded the bicycle as a children's means of getting to and from school, a youngster's plaything, or

IN GEBRUIK BIJ HET NEDERLANDSCHE
EN NEDERLANDSCH INDISCHE LEGER

Manufacturers in many countries suggested and promoted military uses for bicycles from the 1880s until World War II. This was an almost life-size placard printed in 1915 for Fongers bicycles, made in the Netherlands. In English translation, the lines at the bottom proclaim: "Used in the Dutch and Dutch-Indian Army."

a low-cost short-trip vehicle and nothing more. The poet W. H. Auden perfectly described the image of the typical adult rider: "She'd a bicycle with a shopping basket / And a harsh back-pedal brake."

After World War I, the popularity of recreational bicycling for adults diminished, particularly in the United States—in large part supplanted by the automobile—although even in this country both indoor and outdoor racing retained a fairly large and steady following.

The tremendous resurgence of cycling began in the 1970s, and many authorities ascribe the rebirth of the trend, at least in large part, to the astounding influence of one man, Dr. Paul Dudley White, a world-famous cardiologist who campaigned vigorously during the two decades before his death in 1975 for safe bicycle paths and for cycling as an aid to fitness and longevity.

Author of *Cycling in the School Fitness Program*, Dr. White was for many years honorary president of the American Bicycle Hall of Fame, which was founded in 1959 by the Century Road Club Association of New York and, under the New York State Board of

Regents, established a non-profit educational museum at Richmondtown, where the Staten Island Historical Society generously donated a large hall in the Richmondtown Historical Museum.

YESTERDAY'S HEROES, TOMORROW'S HORIZONS

Many famous people have been cyclists, and in a few cases their interest in bicycles had effects reaching far beyond their personal pleasure and fitness. The brothers Orville and Wilbur Wright furnish the most familiar and perhaps most important example. At their Dayton, Ohio, shop, the Wrights designed and built bicycles. When they achieved the first powered, sustained, and controlled airplane flight in 1903, they made use of structural principles they had learned while building light, strong, controllable bikes.

The achievements of a number of less famous people have been memorialized by their election to the American Bicycle Hall of Fame, and a few of the most outstanding names may be of particular interest to readers of this book.

Albert A. Pope (1843-1909) was the first major American bicycle manufacturer and a leading pioneer in the Good Roads Campaign which resulted in nationwide road expansion and improvement.

Thomas Stevens (1854-1935) was the first cyclist to pedal "around the world"—from San Francisco to Boston and then across England, Europe, and Asia. He began pedaling in April, 1884, and finished in Yokohama in December, 1886. And he did it on a high-wheel boneshaker!

A special correspondent for *Outing* magazine, he reported his adventure in that periodical and then gathered the narratives into a popular book, *Around the World on a Bicycle*.

Arthur A. Zimmerman (1869-1936), considered the fastest sprinter of all time (prior to the introduction of today's aerodynamic, ultralight racing bikes), was to bicycle racing what Babe Ruth later was to baseball. At the age of 23, he had won over 1,400 races, earned world renown, and made his preferred bike, the Raleigh Road Racer, famous. In an age of colorful, often undisciplined athletes, this young New Yorker was among the most colorful. He enjoyed the company of Toulouse-Lautrec and other artists, with whom he was likely to stay up all night before a big race, chatting and smoking cigars. Ironically in view of his unorthodox habits,

Thomas Stevens

KELLY .87

This 1887 engraving shows Thomas Stevens, special correspondent for *Outing,* on his round-the-world tour. Riding eastward from San Francisco, he cycled across the United States, Europe, and Asia—the first person to do so—and he did it on a high-wheel boneshaker!

Outing
SPECIAL BICYCLE NUMBER

In 1896, *Outing* magazine, one of the most popular recreational publications of the era, published a special bicycle issue. Ribbons trailed from the woman's handlebar, just as plastic streamers and pompons often do today (and they're still not a smart idea). Few modern riders realize that bikes like those depicted had just about all the basic features found on typical bikes today.

This poster was printed in 1893, shortly after Arthur A. Zimmerman became Champion of the World. By then he had won over 1,400 races. (The figure of 2,300 on the advertisement refers to prizes captured by all the top competitors using Raleigh bicycles.) Zimmerman helped to make the Raleigh Road Racer world famous.

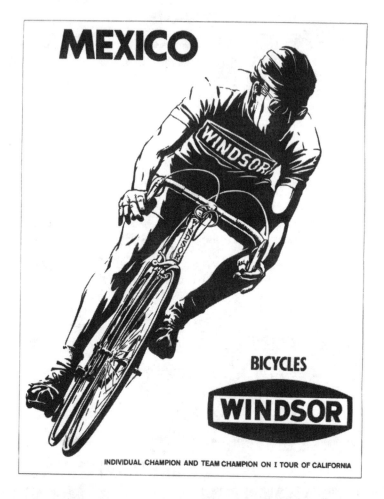

INDIVIDUAL CHAMPION AND TEAM CHAMPION ON I TOUR OF CALIFORNIA

When the Mexican firm of Acer-Mex began producing bicycles shortly after World War II, perhaps the brand name Windsor was chosen for its appeal to two major markets, the United States and Canada. This 1971 advertisement called attention to both the individual and team victories of Windsor riders in the Tour of California race.

he was the author of *Points for Cyclists with Training.*

In 1895, a sportswriter commented that races had become too numerous and bemoaned "the old days" when there were fewer races, fewer competitors, and "to be a Zimmerman was to be better-known than the

President of the United States."

Marshall Taylor (1878-1932) became world champion in 1899 and was author of *The Fastest Bicycle Rider in the World.* He has been called the greatest black cyclist of all time.

Frank Kramer (1880-1958) won the Grand Prix de Paris in 1905 and became world sprint champion in 1912.

Adolph R. Jacobson (1890-1950) founded the Amateur Bicycle League of America, and became the quarter-mile record holder in 1910.

Monroe Smith (1901-1972) was founder, with his wife Isabel, of the American Youth Hostels, a nationwide organization of and for cyclists, hikers, and other outdoor-recreation enthusiasts.

Audrey McElmury, holder of several national championships, became the first American woman to win the World Road Championship in 1969.

Such athletes are rare, and the joys of cycling do not, of course, depend on emulating them. You may not be a contender in the local road races or velodrome, yet your own horizons widen when you get on your bike because the possibilities for relaxation and adventure are always new. You have scores of unexplored miles before you, as H. G. Wells suggested, and as Oliver Wendell Holmes observed, you have wings on your feet.

APPENDIX

I

Clubs and Associations

Various clubs and associations have sprung up to serve the needs and interests of bicycle riders. Some are specialized, like the National Off-Road Bicycle Association (NORBA); and some, like the League of American Wheelmen (LAW), have members whose only common link may be a bicycle. You can write or call the organizations below for more information.

Bicycle Institute of America
  (BIA)
1818 R St., NW
Washington, DC 20009
(202) 332-6986 /
  fax (202) 332-6989

International Mountain Bicycling
  Association (IMBA)
P.O. Box 412043
Los Angeles, CA 90041
(818) 792-8830 / fax (818) 796-
  2299

League of American Wheelmen
  (LAW)
190 W. Ostend St., Suite 120
Baltimore, MD 21230
(410) 539-3399

National Off-Road Bicycle
  Association (NORBA)
1750 E. Boulder St.
Colorado Springs, CO 80909
(719) 578-4717 / fax (719) 578-
  4596

United States Cycling Federation (USCF)
1750 East Boulder St.
Colorado Springs, CO 80909
(719) 578-4581

Women's Mountain Biking and
  Tea Society (WOMBATS)
P.O. Box 757
Fairfax, CA 94930

II

Map and Information Sources

Touring

Touring can take you where you've never been, and even when you tour in areas with which you're familiar there's always a turn that looks enticing, but isn't on your original route. So maps are important. In Chapter 7, I stated that I usually use AAA road maps, and have used maps from Bikecentennial, a non-profit organization that has mapped over 20,000 miles of routes.

Although the American Automobile Association (AAA) is primarily an association for car drivers, their maps detail roads well. Consult your local chapter (listed in your phone directory) for information regarding membership. Maps are free to members. Non-members can purchase them at low cost.

For information about Bikecentennial membership, benefits, and maps, contact:

Bikecentennial
P.O. Box 8308
Missoula, MT 59807
(406) 721-1776

Trail Riding

Trail riding poses a different problem—where can you ride your ATB on trails near your home? Maps are getting more common, but still have some way to go. Ask at a local bike shop or outdoor equipment shop. The local library and bookstores may have books with maps of local trails. In just the last couple of years, quite a few regional bike-touring guide books have been published. Chambers of commerce often have information. Most state and national parks that permit hiking or mountain biking have maps of their trails. Rails-to-Trails Conservancy is a non-profit organization that pushes for converting abandoned railroad corridors into trails for public use, chiefly hiking and cycling. This is a national organization with state chapters. Write to:

Rails-to-Trails Conservancy
1400 Sixteenth St., NW
Washington, DC 20036

General Information and News

The most popular and information-packed periodical for cyclists is *Bicycling* magazine. To inquire about subscribing, write to the magazine at 33 E. Minor St., Emmaus, PA.

III

Equipment and Catalog Sources

Although there's nothing like having a good, reliable bike shop nearby, mail-order services do have their place. Listed below are excellent catalog houses with which the authors are familiar. There are many others, and most mail-order supply houses are reputable.

Bike Nashbar
4111 Simon Rd.
Youngstown, OH 44512-1343
(216) 782-2244

Campmor
P.O. Box 998
Paramus, NJ 07653
(201) 445-5000

L.L. Bean, Inc.
L.L. St.
Freeport, ME 04033
(800) 221-4221

Performance Bicycle
P.O. Box 2741
Chapel Hill, NC 27515-2741
(800) 727-2433